Learning Resources Centre
WQE Regent Road Campus
Regent Road
 Leicester
LE1 7LW
Tel 0116 2554629

7 Day Loan

Return on or before the date stamped below.
If you return books late you will be charged a fine.

Independence Educational Publishers

First published by Independence Educational Publishers

The Studio, High Green

Great Shelford

Cambridge CB22 5EG

England

© Independence 2018

Copyright

Photocopy licence

ISBN-13: 978 1 86168 789 0

Printed in Great Britain

Zenith Print Group

Contents

Introduction

COPING WITH DEATH is Volume 338 in the **ISSUES** series. The aim of the series is to offer current, diverse information about important issues in our world, from a UK perspective.

ABOUT COPING WITH DEATH

Death is a very sensitive subject and one which many people do not like to think or talk about. Very few of us have given thought to where we might like to die when the time comes. Only around two in five adults have written a will. This book explores the many issues which surround death. It looks at ways in which we might plan for our death, the cost of a funeral and explores different funeral rites throughout the world. It also explores the ways in which grief affects people and the help which is available to them.

OUR SOURCES

Titles in the **ISSUES** series are designed to function as educational resource books, providing a balanced overview of a specific subject.

The information in our books is comprised of facts, articles and opinions from many different sources, including:

⇨ Newspaper reports and opinion pieces

⇨ Website factsheets

⇨ Magazine and journal articles

⇨ Statistics and surveys

⇨ Government reports

⇨ Literature from special interest groups.

A NOTE ON CRITICAL EVALUATION

Because the information reprinted here is from a number of different sources, readers should bear in mind the origin of the text and whether the source is likely to have a particular bias when presenting information (or when conducting their research). It is hoped that, as you read about the many aspects of the issues explored in this book, you will critically evaluate the information presented.

It is important that you decide whether you are being presented with facts or opinions. Does the writer give a biased or unbiased report? If an opinion is being expressed, do you agree with the writer? Is there potential bias to the 'facts' or statistics behind an article?

ASSIGNMENTS

In the back of this book, you will find a selection of assignments designed to help you engage with the articles you have been reading and to explore your own opinions. Some tasks will take longer than others and there is a mixture of design, writing and research-based activities that you can complete alone or in a group.

Useful weblinks

www.churchtimes.co.uk

www.theconversation.com

www.finder.com

www.funeralzone.co.uk

www.greenfieldcoffins.co.uk

www.healthtalk.org

www.huffingtonpost.co.uk

www.independent.co.uk

www.iscafunerals.co.uk

www.macmillan.org.uk

www.moneywise.co.uk

www.nhs.uk

www.telegraph.co.uk

www.theguardian.com

www.scattering-ashes.co.uk

www.sunlife.co.uk

FURTHER RESEARCH

At the end of each article we have listed its source and a website that you can visit if you would like to conduct your own research. Please remember to critically evaluate any sources that you consult and consider whether the information you are viewing is accurate and unbiased.

Life expectancy in Britain has fallen so much that a million years of life could disappear by 2058 – why?

THE CONVERSATION

An article from **The Conversation.**

By Danny Dorling, Halford Mackinder Professor of Geography, University of Oxford and Stuart Gietel-Basten, Associate Professor of Social Science and Public Policy, Hong Kong University of Science and Technology

Buried deep in a note towards the end of a recent bulletin published by the British Government's statistical agency was a startling revelation. On average, people in the UK are now projected to live shorter lives than previously thought.

In their projections, published in October 2017, statisticians at the Office for National Statistics (ONS) estimated that by 2041, life expectancy for women would be 86.2 years and 83.4 years for men. In both cases, that's almost a whole year less than had been projected just two years earlier. And the statisticians said life expectancy would only continue to creep upwards in future.

As a result, and looking further ahead, a further one million earlier deaths are now projected to happen across the UK in the next 40 years by 2058. This number was not highlighted in the report. But it jumped out at us when we analysed the tables of projections published alongside it.

It means that the 110 years of steadily improving life expectancy in the UK are now officially over. The implications for this are huge and the reasons the statistics were revised is a tragedy on an enormous scale.

A rising tide of life

Life expectancy is most commonly calculated from birth. It is the average number of years a new-born baby can expect to live if the mortality rates pertaining at the time of their birth apply throughout their life.

In 1891, life expectancy for women in England and Wales was 48 years. For men it was 44. Many people lived longer than this, but so many babies died in their first year of life that, from birth, you were doing better than average if you made it past your forties. For most of the 1890s the Conservatives were in power under Lord Salisbury. They continued to support and build on public health reforms from earlier years, such as the construction of sewers and improvements to the supply of clean piped water. Often these reforms were instigated by local government, which was able to be more proactive than it is today. Adult health improved and by 1901, on average, women lived to 52 and men 48.

The turn of the century saw the start of dramatic improvements in infant mortality as everyday sanitation became paramount and the condition and living standards of mothers started being taken more seriously. The Liberal prime ministers Henry Campbell-Bannerman, Herbert Henry Asquith and David Lloyd George were in charge as most of these improvements occurred. These ranged from the recognition and widespread acceptance that germs cause disease through to the provision of better insurance and pensions, paid for by more progressive taxation. By 1921, women lived to 60 and men to 56.

Life expectancy continued to soar ahead. By 1951, 30 years later, women lived to 72 and men to 66. It rose by more than a year every three years at this time, despite World War II, rationing and 1940's and 1950's austerity. Back then we really were all in it together. For women, better maternity care and the fact that most did not smoke had given them the edge.

Improvements in life expectancy slowed in the 1950s under the Conservative government of Harold Macmillan. To be fair, most of the easy early wins had been achieved, such as clean water supplies and free access to health care at the point of delivery with the introduction of the NHS in 1948. Still, Macmillan tried to pretend that deaths from smog in London were due to influenza. The Conservatives were never able to achieve anything as impressive for public health as Labour's launch of the NHS, which had an immediate effect simply by boosting national morale and access to care, and on infant health. Despite that, and with some help from the policies of Harold Wilson's first Labour Government in the 1960s, by 1971 women lived to 75 and men to 69. This improvement was driven by more spending on health services,

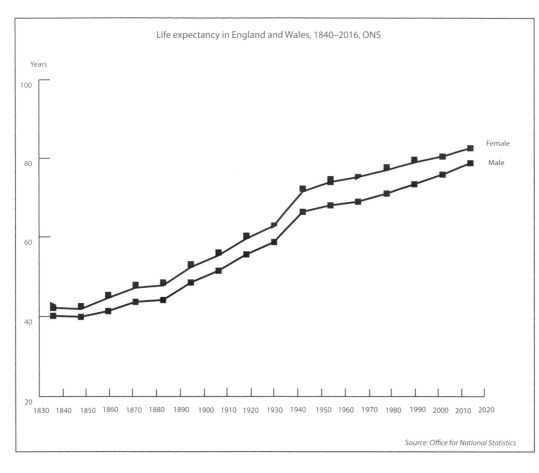

Life expectancy in England and Wales, 1840–2016, ONS

Years

Female
Male

Source: Office for National Statistics

Projections are not predictions

Population estimates are always hard to make and even harder to explain. In 1990, in *The New York Review of Books*, the economist Amartya Sen wrote that: 'More than 100 million women are missing' in the world. Sen wrote that compared to men in Europe and North America:

'The fate of women is quite different in most of Asia and North Africa. In these places the failure to give women medical care similar to what men get and to provide them with comparable food and social services results in fewer women surviving than would be the case if they had equal care.'

There is some irony that a quarter of a century later we now have to ask why, in one of the richest countries in the world, are we now not expecting people to enjoy as long a life as we were expecting them to just two years ago?

The Government accepts that air pollution already contributes to around 40,000 premature deaths a year. Why then is there not more public outrage when an additional 39,307 deaths occurred in the year up until June 2017 than had been expected?

And it happened the year after an additional 30,000 people had already died in 2015.

In November 2017, the ONS went on to project that there will be more than an extra 25,000 deaths between July 2017 and June 2018. Then an extra 27,000 deaths in the 12 months after that, more than an extra 28,000 deaths the year after that – and on and on and on. It now looks as if we should come to expect heightened mortality year after year until the end of our lives.

The Government has given no reason for why this is happening. But there is absolutely no reason to suppose that this is due to something beyond our control.

Whatever has happened it is not a sudden worsening of the healthy behaviour of people in the UK. It is not a sudden rise in obesity or some additional carelessness about looking after ourselves. Neither obesity nor any other human behaviour linked to poor health such as smoking or drinking alcohol has seen a sudden rise. In fact, health complaints from smoking have plummeted since the introduction of the 2007 ban on

smoking in public places. The number of Britons who smoke is at its lowest level.

The proportion of adults who drink alcohol in the UK is also currently at its lowest level since 2005. Obesity is still rising, but it has been for decades now, and the age groups now dying in high numbers – the over-80s – are not yet those who became obese in recent decades.

The most likely culprit, by far, is austerity, including the effect of the cuts to social and healthcare services.

We will not live longer by all taking responsibility just for ourselves alone, looking after just us and our families, trying to get fitter, eat better and worry less. This is not how the health of whole nations improves. It is about all of us, not just one of us. That is why it is a million years of life. And we should not allow that million to be announced quietly, like the inevitable dying of the light.

As we argue in our new book, demography is not destiny. Projections are not predictions. There is no preordained inevitability that a million years of life need be lost, but already, 120,000 have been by 2017.

The rest of those million early deaths could be avoided. There is no biological reason why life expectancy should be so low in the UK compared to almost all other affluent nations. The social sciences and epidemiologists between them have the answers, but only through politics comes the power to make the changes that are now so urgently needed.

29 November 2017

⇨ The above information is reprinted with kind permission from *The Conversation*. Please visit www. theconversation.com for further information.

Health statistics

How healthy is the UK?

We have compiled all the latest stats to give you an insight into the health of the UK.

General health of the UK

⇨ **Life expectancy.** 82.3 years for men and 85.8 years for women.

⇨ **Healthy life expectancy.** The age up to which people can expect to live healthily is 63.1 for men and 63.7 for women.

⇨ **UK health spending.** £185 billion was spent on healthcare by government and privately, up 3.6% in 2014.

⇨ **Per person health spending.** Per capita spending of £3,377.

⇨ **Obesity.** 26% of adults in the UK are obese.

⇨ **Deaths.** 525,000 deaths in the UK in 2016.

Death statistics in the UK

Ultimately a factor of life, we look into the stats for deaths in the UK in the last year. There were over 520,000 deaths in the UK in 2016, although this sounds bleak, it does represent a decline of 0.9% from 2015.

525,048

deaths registered in the UK in 2016, down 0.9% from 2015.

The top causes of death in the UK were the following:

⇨ Dementia and Alzheimer disease.

⇨ Ischaemic heart diseases.

⇨ Cerebrovascular diseases.

⇨ Chronic lower respiratory diseases.

⇨ Lung cancer.

12%

of deaths in the UK were caused by Dementia and Alzheimer disease, up 0.4% from 2015.

Alcohol consumption

It's no secret that the UK has a strong drinking culture – but just how much of a problem is it?

⇨ 1,100,000: alcohol-related admissions to the NHS, up 4% from 2014/15.

⇨ Almost two-thirds: of alcohol-related admissions were male.

⇨ 7,327: alcohol-specific deaths in 2016.

⇨ 55%: on average, alcohol related deaths are 55% higher for men than women.

⇨ Scotland: has the highest deaths of any region,

but have fallen 21% from 2001 to 2016.

⇨ 57%: of the UK population drink alcohol.

But how do these figures stack up against the rest of Europe? See Table 2.

How bad are obesity figures in the UK?

26% of UK adults are obese according to recent government reports. The stats below explore just how bad obesity figures in the UK are.

⇨ 58% of women were obese or overweight.

⇨ 68% of men were obese or overweight.

⇨ 1 in 5 children in Reception were obese or overweight.

⇨ 1 in 3 children in Year 6 were obese or overweight.

⇨ 525,000 admissions to the NHS where obesity was recorded as a factor.

⇨ 26% of adults are obese.

Table 1		
Life expectancy has increased for both males and females since 2001–2003		
Gender	Year	Life expectancy
Males	2001–2003	78.8 years
Males	2014–2016	82.3 years
Females	2001–2003	83.3 years
Females	2014–2016	85.8 years

Source: Finder

Table 2		
Rank	Country	Consumption (Litres/Capita, aged 15 and older)
1	France	11.9
2	Czech Republic	11.5
3	Slovenia	11.5
4	Ireland	10.9
5	Latvia	10.8
6	Poland	10.5
7	Estonia	10.3
8	Slovak Republic	10.2
9	United Kingdom	9.5
10	Finland	8.5

Source: Finder

£42.43

average spend on food and drink, per person, per week.

Work-related accidents

See the details of work-related accidents in 2016.

⇨ 609,000: injuries occurred at work.

⇨ 31.2 million: days lost to workplace injuries.

⇨ £14.9 billion: estimated loss due to workplace injury or sickness.

⇨ 137: workers killed in 2016.

⇨ 62%: of injuries at work were to men.

609,000

injuries occurred at the workplace in 2016.

Mental health

Major depression is thought to be the second leading cause of disability worldwide and a major contributor to the burden of suicide and ischaemic heart disease. Below are some more stats regarding mental health in the UK.

One in six people experienced a common mental health problem within the last week.

⇨ 5,965 suicides in the UK in 2016, down 3.6% from 2015.

⇨ 75%, almost three-quarters of these suicides were men.

3.6%

fewer suicides in 2016 than in 2015.

15 February 2018

⇨ The above information is reprinted with kind permission from Finder UK. Please visit www.finder.com for further information.

No regrets

An extract from *How talking more openly about death could help people die well.*

By Adriene Betteley, PG Dip Res, BSC (Hons) Specialist Practitioner District Nursing, RN (Adult) Head of Health and Social Care, Macmillan Cancer Support

The problem with talking

Death and cancer as 'taboo' subjects

Our research has identified that there is still a considerable taboo around talking about death, and also talking about cancer.

For those who are faced with illness, death may be a sensitive topic, and something that they do not want to face just yet. For others, it may seem far off and irrelevant to them – or, so inevitable and out of their control that there is no point thinking about it, let alone having conversations about it.

When we surveyed the general public, one in seven people (15%) opted out of answering questions about death. This figure rises to 26% among young men. It seems that for some, it may be a topic that they simply don't want to think about, or which they do not feel is relevant to them. Fear may be a big part of this.

Of the people we surveyed, the vast majority (84%) had fears about death.

We found that 94% of people living with cancer answered our questions relating to death. This could be because they have been faced with the prospect of their own death.

Around three in four (76%) had thought about the fact that they might die from their cancer.

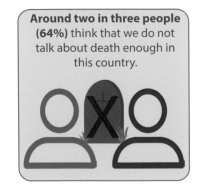

Around two in three people (64%) think that we do not talk about death enough in this country.

But despite this, there was reluctance to voice these concerns. Just over a third (35%) of people who said they had thoughts and feelings about their death had not shared these feelings with anyone. Only 8% had spoken to their healthcare team.

When asked why they hadn't shared their worries with anyone, a fifth (20%) said that they didn't feel comfortable talking about it and around one in five (22%) said that they didn't want to bother anyone.

More than one in four people with cancer (28%) find it hard to be honest about how they feel about cancer.

Rhys' story

Being able to talk about death, rather than avoiding the reality of it, can be vital, as Rhys' experience shows.

Rhys, 38, was living with his girlfriend Rhea and working as a bartender in Manchester, hoping to go to university to complete a PhD, when he was diagnosed with terminal lung adenocarcinoma in July 2015. In April 2016, Rhea and Rhys got married.

"No one has ever discussed making plans with me. No one has even barely discussed the fact that I'm dying. From diagnosis, all the way up to now, there's a total avoidance of the idea that you might not actually make it – even though the consultant is there telling you it's terminal." Rhys

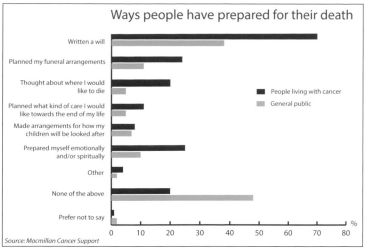

Ways people have prepared for their death

- Written a will
- Planned my funeral arrangements
- Thought about where I would like to die
- Planned what kind of care I would like towards the end of my life
- Made arrangements for how my children will be looked after
- Prepared myself emotionally and/or spiritually
- Other
- None of the above
- Prefer not to say

■ People living with cancer
■ General public

0 10 20 30 40 50 60 70 80 %

Source: Macmillan Cancer Support

Rhys initially responded well to treatment and lived beyond his initial prognosis. However, his health deteriorated rapidly in October 2016 and in January 2017, Rhys died in hospital with Rhea at his side.

'All of the advice and guidance you get, you have to go and seek it out. It would be so great if a person just came to you and said, "we should talk about this". There are bereavement counsellors, and going back to work counsellors, but there's no 'hey, you're going to die' counsellor.'

Rhys

'We had spoken about what he wanted between us, but we never really put anything formal in place. The whole experience has been really upsetting.'

Rhea, Rhys' wife

Planning a good death

So why is the taboo around death and dying important? It's because there is a vast difference between a 'good' and a 'bad' death – both to the individual and the people they have left behind.

We asked people with cancer where they would like to die, if they had the right care and support:

⇨ 64% of people with cancer would like to die at home; only 30% currently do.

⇨ Only 1% stated a hospital as their preferred place; 38% of people currently die in hospital.

By making it more natural to talk about death, it will be less difficult to have those vital conversations about what someone's final wishes are. If concerns and preferences about care are raised early enough, a lot can be done to make sure they are dealt with. This is what happened with Peter.

"When you see someone die in the way you know they want; it can be empowering. If only people could see that a death could be a good one, they would be a lot more passionate about it."

Macmillan clinical nurse specialist, Palliative Care

Peter's story

Peter, 81, was diagnosed with incurable lung mesothelioma – an asbestos-related cancer – in July 2016 after suffering from chest pains.

He was put in touch with the local hospice who began to work through an Advance Care Plan with him and his daughter, Vivien.

'I told him I wasn't scared of dying but I was apprehensive about dying in pain.'

Peter

He died in November 2016 having fulfilled his wish not to die in pain.

'It was great because it didn't leave anything unsaid and brought us closer together. I knew exactly what he wanted and what he was scared of so when it came to the end I knew that he got what he wanted and it made things easier for me to cope with.'

Vivien, Peter's daughter

Peter's story is an example of the value of talking about death. Speaking with his healthcare team and with his daughter about his priorities meant that they could focus on fulfilling his wishes. For Vivien, it helped her cope emotionally with her father's death.

Make planning normal

Across our research, many people were undertaking various levels of planning around their death. Around two in five members of the public (38%) have written a will, and 70% of people with cancer have done so. Rhys, whose story is mentioned earlier, married Rhea in preparation for his death.

Our survey of the general public found that just one in 20 people (5%) have thought about where they would like to die, and only 5% have planned their future care.

Among people with cancer, these figures are higher, but still much lower than those who have made a will. One in five (20%) have thought about where they would like to die, and one in nine (11%) have planned their future care.

Thinking or talking about death, and making plans for it, isn't giving up. In fact, it is taking control of a situation that is otherwise out of your control.

Dying is too important to be left to the end. Dying is a part of life, and one which is – to some extent – in our control.

People also need to be made aware that:

⇨ a 'good' death is possible

⇨ they do have choices around their future care

⇨ with early conversations, these can be managed.

April 2017

⇨ The above extract is reprinted with kind permission from Macmillan Cancer Support. Please visit www.macmillan.org.uk for further information.

© 2018 Macmillan Cancer Support

We fear death, but what if dying isn't as bad as we think?

Research comparing perceptions of death with accounts of those imminently facing it suggest that maybe we shouldn't worry so much about our own end.

By Jessica E. Brown

'The idea of death, the fear of it, haunts the human animal like nothing else,' wrote Earnest Becker in his book, The Denial of Death. It's a fear strong enough to compel us to force kale down our throats, run sweatily on a treadmill at 7am on a Monday morning, and show our genitals to a stranger with cold hands and a white coat if we feel something's a little off.

But our impending end isn't just a benevolent supplier of healthy behaviours. Researchers have found death can determine our prejudices, whether we give to charity or wear sun cream, our desire to be famous, what type of leader we vote for, how we name our children and even how we feel about breastfeeding.

And, of course, it terrifies us. Death anxiety appears to be at the core of several mental health disorders, including health anxiety, panic disorder and depressive disorders. And we're too scared to talk about it. A ComRes survey from 2014 found that eight in ten Brits are uncomfortable talking about death, and only a third have written a will.

But we don't need to worry so much, according to new research comparing our perception of what it's like to die with the accounts of people facing imminent death. Researchers analysed the writing of regular bloggers with either terminal cancer or amyotrophic lateral sclerosis (ALS) who all died over the course of the study, and compared it to blog posts written by a group of participants who were told to imagine they had been diagnosed with terminal cancer and had only a few months to live. They looked for general feelings of positivity and negativity, and words describing positive and negative emotions including happiness, fear and terror.

Blog posts from the terminally ill were found to have considerably more positive words and fewer negative ones than those imagining they were dying – and their use of positive language increased as they got close to death.

Kurt Gray, one of the study's researchers, said, 'I imagine this is because they know things are getting more serious, and there's some kind of acceptance and focusing on the positive because they know they don't have a lot of time left.'

The researchers also compared the last words and poetry of inmates on death row with a group of people tasked with imagining they were about to face execution. Again, there were fewer negative words from the prisoners. Overall, those facing death focused more on what makes life meaningful, including family and religion.

'We talk all the time about how physically adaptable we are, but we're also mentally adaptable. We can be happy in prison, in hospital, and we can be happy at the edge of death as well,' Gray said.

'Dying isn't just part of the human condition, but central to it. Everyone dies, and most of us are afraid of it. Our study is important because it's saying this isn't as universally bad as we think it is'.

But before we get too ahead of ourselves, the research prompts a few questions. Lisa Iverach, a research fellow at the University of Sydney, explained that the study highlights how the participants may have been less negative because the mystery around death was removed.

'Individuals facing imminent death have had more time to process the idea of death and dying, and therefore, may be more accepting of the inevitability of death. They also have a very good idea about how they are going to die, which may bring some sense of peace or acceptance.'

But not all of us will know how, or when, we're going to die in advance of it happening, and therefore will miss out on any benefits to be had by uncovering its uncertainty.

Havi Carel, Professor of Philosophy at the University of Bristol, agrees with the study's findings on how adaptable we are. 'I think you get used to the idea of dying, like we get accustomed to many things. The initial shock after receiving a poor prognosis is horrific, but after months or years of living with this knowledge, the dread subsides,' she said.

However, Carel also pointed out that there's an important distinction between positive responses and pleasantness, and that there are some unpleasant and painful events we'd still be positive about, such as childbirth.

'Blogs are written for public consumption and they remain there after people's death. Using blogs and poetry may reveal only the outward-

facing emotions people are willing to share, or even simply created to fashion how they want to be remembered. Do people really tell the truth in their blogs? Perhaps, to an extent, but these are very public media,' Carel said.

'Perhaps they are 'putting on a brave face'. It is impossible to tell, but blogs are clearly not the most intimate mode of communication. It may have been better to use diaries, recorded conversations with loved ones, or even personal letters.'

Nathan Heflick, researcher and lecturer at the University of Lincoln, also warns against interpreting the results to mean that dying people view death as a wholly positive experience. 'I think that is a dangerous message, and it isn't a conclusion reflected in the study's data. Being less negative is different from welcoming it or wanting death,' he said.

'People will fear death. These people dying feared death. They just didn't fear it as much as people think they would.'

If fear of death is, in fact, as inevitable as the event itself – there's one change we can make to help. In Western culture, we tend to pretend death doesn't exist, whereas research has indicated that the East Asian yin and yang philosophy of death – where life can't exist without death – allows individuals to use death as a reminder to enjoy life.

'I think the UK and the US are death-denying cultures, in that death is mostly avoided as a topic,' Heflick said.

'The less something is openly discussed, the scarier it becomes. While avoiding talking about death can reduce a little discomfort in the short term, it probably makes most of us much more anxious about dying in the long term.'

25 July 2017

⇨ The above information is reprinted with kind permission from *The Guardian*. Please visit www.theguardian.com for further information.

CuddleCots: invention allows parents of stillborn children to spend more time with them

For many grieving parents, a CuddleCot can mean spending a few more days with the baby they carried for nine months.

By Olivia Blair

When a baby is born stillborn, parents can sometimes only have a few hours to spend time with their child and say goodbye.

The amount of time parents can spend with a stillborn is usually restricted because the body of the infant can deteriorate in warm rooms, especially if it has been dead for a few days.

Flexmort developed the CuddleCot – a cot which cools the baby and therefore prolongs the amount of time parents can spend with their stillborn infant – in 2011.

Simon Rothwell, a founder of Cuddle-Cot and former policeman, started the company after previously working on cooling devices for deceased obese people and then visiting children's hospices where bodies tended to be kept in cold rooms along with the parents who would stay for days with a deceased child, while being extremely cold themselves.

In hospitals, the CuddleCot might allow the parents to spend a night with the baby. However, if the mother has had a traumatic labour and has been unable to see their baby for a few days this might be longer. Mr Rothwell says how long the baby can be kept in the CuddleCot depends on a number of variables including when the baby died and how often it has been taken out of the cot. He is aware of a family who kept their baby for a few weeks over Christmas because they did not want to be apart from it at that time of year.

'They have carried a baby for nine months generally and the only time and memories they will get will be for that day or two,' Mr Rothwell told *The Independent*. 'So, it's absolutely so important for families and it really does help them. The feedback we get has been phenomenally positive.'

The frequent use of CuddleCots has mainly happened through word-of-

mouth, which Mr Rothwell says is good considering the "horrific" nature of the topic the product caters to. They are used in 92 per cent of hospitals in the UK as well as hospitals and children's hospices in the USA, Canada and New Zealand. The hospitals tend to buy them from Flexmort who then provide them for free to the families.

'Most hospitals will offer families the choice. The difficult part is that stillborns are quite common and there might be two people at the hospital that need one yet only one can get it.'

Mel gave birth to her stillborn baby, Finley, in 2009 after undergoing an emergency caesarian when his heart rate dropped. At the time, a CuddleCot was not available but being as though Finley died minutes before birth, he did not deteriorate quickly so Mel and her partner were able to spend three days with him in a bereavement suite.

'Though we didn't know what was possible, what we could do, the staff were fantastic making suggestions and supporting us,' Mel told *The Independent*. 'We have photographs and videos from this time. We changed him, he stayed with us the whole three days. We have footprints, and casts, gave him gifts and dressed him in different outfits.

'The bereavement midwife helped me to prepare to say goodbye. She asked me what I wanted my last memory to be, and took photographs of us on our last night, suggested I kiss my son and didn't bat an eyelid when I broke down and explained that I wanted

to change his nappy… All these things have helped us so much. The memories have made Finley real, tangible to other people, and our time with him was so precious.'

Mel later raised money to provide a CuddleCot for the Musgrove Park hospital in Taunton who helped her so much through her own trauma. She has also set up a charity, Towards Tomorrow Together which supports grieving parents of stillborn babies in the West Midlands and Somerset, saying she always recommends CuddleCots.

'I have known parents who have been able to see their baby after being seriously unwell and unconscious for a number of days. The CuddleCot is particularly helpful for babies born at an earlier gestation, or who have been dead for a number of number days. These families ordinarily may only be able to spend a few hours before the baby deteriorates too much, meaning that things have to happen so quickly… It is a key piece of equipment in supporting families after the loss of a baby, allowing extra time, slowing

down the necessity to make decisions quickly, which they may regret, and allowing more families the chance to take their baby home to grieve in their own way.'

Recently, a couple used a CuddleCot for 16 days to grieve for their baby. Charlotte Szakacs, 21, told *The Telegraph*: 'I know it might not be the best option for everyone but for us it was so important to be able to have that family time… I think having the time with her made such a difference. Being able to do so many of the things you imagine like taking her out in her pram, it really helped emotionally.'

Mr Rothwell said despite the incredibly personal nature of using a CuddleCot, sometimes the company and parents become victims of trolling.

'The trolling that goes on sometimes is just horrible,' Mr Rothwell says. 'Our experience is generally positive because people who have been through it or work in these areas realise how important it is for the family… you just see it online sometimes

with people trolling it saying it is 'disgusting'. You don't know, you've never walked in their shoes.'

Erica Stewart, bereavement support and awareness specialist at Sands stillbirth and neonatal death charity, told *The Independent* the CuddleCot is an option chosen by many parents.

'When a baby dies it's a huge shock and there is only a small window of time for bereaved parents to create memories. One of the things they may be offered is the use of a CuddleCot. Many parents choose this option as it allows them to spend longer, precious extra time with their baby.'

4 April 2017

⇨ The above information is reprinted with kind permission from *The Independent*. Please visit www.independent.co.uk for further information.

© independent.co.uk 2018

Girl, 14, who died of cancer cryogenically frozen after telling judge she wanted to be brought back to life 'in hundreds of years'

By Gordon Rayner, Chief Reporter

A 14-year-old girl who died of cancer has been cryogenically frozen in the hope that she can be 'woken up' and cured in the future after winning a landmark court case in her final days.

The girl's divorced parents had disagreed over whether her wish to be frozen should be followed, so the girl, who cannot be named for legal reasons, asked a High Court judge to intervene.

In a heartbreaking letter to the court, she said: 'I don't want to die but I know I am going to... I want to live longer... I want to have this chance.'

The girl, known as JS, asked Mr Justice Peter Jackson to rule that her mother, who supported her desire to be cryogenically preserved, should be the only person allowed to make decisions about the disposal of her body.

Shortly before her death in a London hospital on 17 October, in what is believed to be a unique case, the judge granted JS her wish. Her body was frozen and taken to a storage facility in the US. She is one of only ten Britons to have been frozen, and the only British child.

She told a relative: 'I'm dying, but I'm going to come back again in 200 years.'

But after a decision that raises profound moral and ethical questions, the judge and the girl's doctors expressed serious misgivings about the process, which did not go entirely according to plan. Her mother spent the last hours of her daughter's life fretting about details of the freezing process, which was 'disorganised' and caused 'real concern' to hospital staff.

The judge suggested that 'proper regulation' of cryonic preservation – which is currently legal but unregulated should now be considered.

Cryogenic preservation of bodies does not fall under the remit of the Human Tissue Authority, which regulates the safe and ethical use of human tissue and organs, because it was 'not contemplated' when the Human Tissue Act 2004 was passed.

Cryonics UK, the non-profit organisation that prepared the girl's body for transport to the US, agreed with the judge.

A spokesman for the firm said: 'We expect that future regulation will help hospitals to know where they stand legally and procedurally. The opportunity to utilise professional medical assistance may increase as we become a recognised and regulated field.'

The case can only now be reported because Mr Justice Jackson ruled that nothing could be published until one month after JS's death. He also ruled that her parents' names and other specific details should remain secret.

JS, who lived with her mother in London, was diagnosed with a rare form of cancer last year and by August this year she had been told her illness was terminal and active treatment came to an end.

She began researching cryonic preservation online – a controversial and costly process that involves the freezing of a dead body in the hope that resuscitation and a cure may one day be possible – and decided she wanted to be frozen after her death.

Because she was too young to make a legally recognised will, she had to have the permission of both of her parents to sign up for the process.

When she contacted her father, whom she has not seen since 2008 and who himself has cancer, he said he was opposed to the idea, so JS began legal proceedings through a solicitor to ensure her wishes were followed.

She was too ill to attend court, but wrote: 'I think being cryo-preserved gives me a chance to be cured and woken up, even in hundreds of years' time. I don't want to be buried underground.

'I want to live and live longer and I think that in the future they might find a cure for my cancer and wake me up.'

On 6 October, the judge ordered that JS's mother should have the sole right to decide what happened to her daughter's body, while stressing that he was not making any ruling about the proposed cryonic preservation.

He also granted an injunction preventing the father from attempting to make any arrangements for the disposal of his daughter's body. He said he had been convinced JS was a 'bright, intelligent young person' with the capacity to bring the application.

JS's parents could not afford to pay for the cryonic process, which costs from £37,000, but her maternal

grandparents raised the money needed for her body to be frozen and taken to a storage facility in America – one of only two countries, along with Russia, that has facilities for storing frozen bodies.

Expressing sympathy with the girl's father, Mr Justice Jackson said: 'No other parent has ever been put in his position. It is no surprise that this application is the only one of its kind to have come before the courts in this country – and probably anywhere else.'

He added: 'It may be thought that the events in this case suggest the need for proper regulation of cryonic preservation in this country if it is to happen in the future.'

How a family tragedy turned into a landmark court case.

As 14-year-old JS lay in hospital, waiting for her terminal cancer to claim her life, she found comfort, and hope, in the idea that science might help her to cheat death.

After spending months online researching the theory of cryonics, the freezing of bodies in the hope that they could one day be brought back to life, JS made up her mind.

'I'm dying, but I'm going to come back again in 200 years,' she told one relative.

Her mother agreed that being cryogenically frozen represented a chance to resume her life once science had found a cure for her cancer.

Her father, however, saw cryonics as a lose-lose proposition. The most likely outcome was that it would not work, in which case his daughter's family would have been put through unnecessary distress and expense.

The alternative, however, was potentially worse, as he set out in a statement to a judge who was to decide his daughter's posthumous fate.

'Even if the treatment is successful and she is brought back to life in, let's say, 200 years,' he said, 'she may not find any relative and she might not remember things.

'She may be left in a desperate situation – given that she is still only 14 years old – and will be in the United States of America [where her body was to be stored].'

The disagreement between mother and father forced JS, who as a minor needed the consent of both parents for the process to be carried out, to seek a court order determining her fate.

The court case which followed not only represented a human and family tragedy, but also shone a light on a little-known and highly controversial industry that describes itself as 'an ambulance to the future'.

Teetering between science fiction and science fact, cryonics is a leap of faith, relying entirely on future medical advances that may or may not happen.

Its proponents frame it as a choice between 'definitely' dying and 'maybe' living on.

JS, described by her teachers as caring, happy and friendly, was diagnosed with a rare form of cancer in August 2015, and despite in-patient treatment at a London hospital, she was told her illness was terminal and in August this year her active treatment was stopped.

By then she had already spent months researching cryonics and, according to court papers, 'pursued her investigations with determination, even though a number of people have tried to dissuade her'.

She chose 'the most basic arrangement' offered by an American company, the Cryonics Institute, one of only three companies in the world that stores frozen bodies. In order to get her body to Michigan, where the company is based, she also contacted Cryonics UK, a non-profit volunteer organisation that offers the country's only cryonic preparation service.

Her parents were far from wealthy, but her maternal grandparents managed to raise the £37,000 that was needed.

There was, however, a problem. JS's father, who had not seen his daughter since 2008 (having applied unsuccessfully through the courts for contact visits), had to be told of her plans and asked to sign parental consent forms. He was reluctant to agree.

He was concerned about the moral and ethical implications of the process, and whether he could be pursued for payments at some point in the future despite living on benefits.

His daughter, with her mother's help, hired a solicitor who applied for the disagreement to be settled by the Family Division of the High Court.

When the case came before Mr Justice Jackson last month, JS's father changed his mind, saying: 'I respect the decisions she is making. This is the last and only thing she has asked from me.'

But he had one condition: that he could see his daughter's body after she died, to say goodbye to the child he had not seen for eight years.

JS and her mother said no, forcing the judge to settle what he described as 'a tragic combination of childhood illness and family conflict'.

Mr Justice Jackson said 'I fully understand the father's misgivings' and pointed out that the girl's doctors felt 'deep unease' about cryonics, making the case 'an example of the new questions that science poses to the law'.

He granted JS's wishes, having noted that 'the prospect of her wishes being followed will reduce her agitation and distress about her impending death'.

Cryonics UK, otherwise known as the Human Organ Preservation Research Trust charity, was put on standby and as JS's condition worsened, a team of four volunteers assembled at the hospital.

Meanwhile Mr Justice Jackson visited JS in hospital, at her request, and said he was 'moved by the valiant way in which she was facing her predicament'.

On 17 October, ten days after the judge's visit, JS 'died peacefully in the knowledge that her body would be preserved in the way she wished'.

However, the judge was sent a note by the hospital which made 'unhappy reading', he said.

On the day JS died, 'her mother is said to have been pre-occupied with the post-mortem arrangements at the expense of being fully available to JS,' said the judge.

'The voluntary organisation is said to have been under-equipped and

disorganised, resulting in pressure being placed on the hospital to allow procedures that had not been agreed.'

The process involves replacing the blood with an anti-freeze fluid, slowly cooling the body to -70° C, and then packing it in dry ice to be transported to a storage facility. Although the preparation of JS's body for cryogenic preservation was completed, 'the way in which the process was handled caused real concern to the medical and mortuary staff', the judge said.

About a week after her death, JS's body was packed into a metal crate with around 40kg of dry ice and loaded onto an aeroplane bound for Michigan, where it will be stored in a vat of liquid nitrogen by the Cryonics Institute at its facility in Clinton Township.

The company, which also stores dead pets, makes no excuse for the fact that it can only offer the 'hope that future medical technology may be able to someday revive and restore them to full health'.

To date, around 350 people have been frozen since the process was invented in the 1960s. Around 20 bodies thawed out and had to be buried after a pioneer company went bust, but the Cryonics Institute and its rival, Arizona-based Alcor, have been storing bodies since the 1970s.

There is no proof that the process of cryo-preservation could ever be reversed.

18 November 2016

⇨ The above information is reprinted with kind permission from *The Telegraph*. Please visit www.telegraph.co.uk for further information.

No longer undone by death

The running of Death Cafes, using the Church of England's GraveTalk material, has had a marked impact on a health trust's work with patients on end-of-life care discovers Pat Ashworth.

Given the choice, most of us would opt to die at home, or in a hospice. Only eight per cent of people expressly want to die in hospital, but statistics show that 54.8 per cent actually do – a figure that indicates not only the importance of end-of-life hospital care, but also the need for a conversation about the many issues surrounding death and dying.

The Revd Ian Dewar is full-time chaplain to the University Hospitals of Morecambe Bay Hospitals NHS Foundation Trust (UHMBT), where care for the dying and bereaved has been deemed outstanding by the Care Quality Commission (CQC). The Trust was rated inadequate in 2014, but inspectors have now rated it as 'Good' overall, with 'Outstanding' for end-of-life care.

Their report highlighted the combined efforts of the bereavement team, chaplaincy, and specialist palliative-care team to promote compassionate care. The introduction of Death Cafés – informal gatherings where people can talk comfortably over tea and cake about death and dying – came in for high praise, especially in relation to how the cafés are helping hospital staff to communicate better with patients and relatives at the end of life.

The concept is based on the Café Mortel movement in Switzerland, and the first Death Café in Britain was set up by Jon Underwood in 2011. Feeling that people had lost control of one of the most significant events they would ever have to face, he wanted to raise awareness, and help people make the most of their finite lives. The movement spread, and some Death Cafés now use the Church of England's pioneering GraveTalk material: 52 question cards that groups can use to start a conversation.

Death Cafés do just what it says on the tin, Mr Dewar says. A hospice chaplain for eight years before taking up his present post three years ago,

he acknowledges that talking about death can be much easier in the hospice context, since the ethos of a hospital is to make people better.

'In a hospice, you have time. In an acute setting, it is very often either a meeting when people have just been delivered the bad news, or the call-out at the point where the bad news is reaching its conclusion,' he says. 'In the first instance, sitting round the bed with the person, and family members, it's OK to say: 'I think the key question to keep in mind is: what will give you the best quality of life?' People appreciate honesty and directness, if delivered sensitively.

'What you mustn't do is bring out clichés and metaphors. Often the look on the face, or the words they use, will give you the clue you want. I try to open up the space and ask whether they'd like me to pray with the person; or, if the person is conscious, I might pray not an end-of-life prayer, but a prayer that they have the strength to face what lies before them.'

Older people can be resilient and honest about facing death, he says. 'My gran had three jars on the mantelpiece: food money, rent money, and funeral money.' But death is a topic spoken about less and less in modern life. 'In the Death Café, we're trying to open the conversation. The way our psyche is at the moment, we have to break through the cultural barrier before we can do that.'

Death Cafés were trialled at Morecambe in early 2016, and were the main focus of the Trust's Dying Matters week in May that year. By the end of 2016, they had also been extended to staff training and community groups.

Mr Dewar has held a Death Café with sixth-formers in a school; the GraveTalk material was used to promote conversations about death, dying, and funerals. The responses were profound, Mr Dewar says. 'One boy said: 'I'm thinking of joining the Army, and wonder whether I can actually [bring myself to] kill someone. I'm going to have to work all this out.' Another commented: 'You don't often get the chance to talk about something, and not feel you have to give an answer at the end.'

Public engagement is a key lesson for end-of-life care, Mr Dewar suggests. 'The difficulty when talking to patients is that it is mostly done in a professional context, and led by a professional; this is, by and large, unavoidable. But it presents a problem: how do you know what people think? How can you gauge what the 'average' non-clinical professional and the 'average' clinical professional may genuinely think, or feel, about death?'

5 May 2017

⇨ The above information is reprinted with kind permission from the *Church Times*. Please visit www.churchtimes.co.uk for further information.

Cost of Dying Report 2017

A complete view of funeral costs over time, 11th edition.

Changes to the average cost of a basic funeral

The cost of a basic funeral, which makes up 46% of the total cost of dying (up from 44% in 2016), has risen by 4.7% from £3,897 in 2016 to £4,078 in 2017.

This figure is calculated by taking the combined average cost of cremations and burials; the average cost of a burial in 2017 is £4,561, which is almost £1,000 (£965) more than the average cost of a cremation – £3,596.

The cost of a burial has risen by 4.7% in the past year and by 116% since SunLife began tracking costs in 2004.

The cost of a religious burial is even higher. The average is £4,715 which is more than two-and-a-half times what it cost in 2004.

If funeral costs continue to rise at the same rate we have seen over the past decade, the average funeral will cost almost £5,000 in five years' time.

Funeral costs are rising almost twice the rate of wages

Funeral costs have seen a 4.7% increase in the past year, and in the past decade, that is a rise of more than 70%.

This may not sound particularly shocking, but when you compare the increase in funeral costs over the past ten years to the increase in other costs – including petrol prices, electricity prices, house prices and weekly wages – the comparison is stark. Over the past decade, funeral costs have increased at more than triple the rate of the others.

If wages had risen in line with funeral costs, the average weekly wage would be £714 today, but in reality, it is £503. And if the cost of bread had risen at the rate of funerals, it would now cost £1.52 for a 800g loaf rather than £1.03.

Even house prices have only risen at a third the rate of funerals; today, the average house price is £223,257, but if house prices had risen in line with funerals, the average home would now cost £94,696 more, an average of £317,953.

How the cost of a basic funeral adds up

The cost of a basic funeral is calculated by adding together the funeral director's

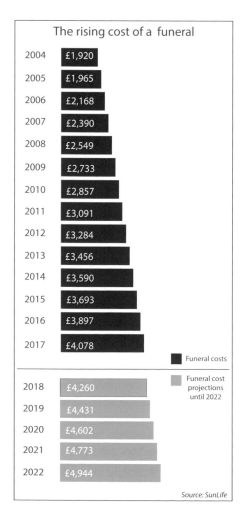

The rising cost of a funeral

Year	Funeral costs
2004	£1,920
2005	£1,965
2006	£2,168
2007	£2,390
2008	£2,549
2009	£2,733
2010	£2,857
2011	£3,091
2012	£3,284
2013	£3,456
2014	£3,590
2015	£3,693
2016	£3,897
2017	£4,078

■ Funeral costs
■ Funeral cost projections until 2022

Year	Funeral cost projections
2018	£4,260
2019	£4,431
2020	£4,602
2021	£4,773
2022	£4,944

Source: SunLife

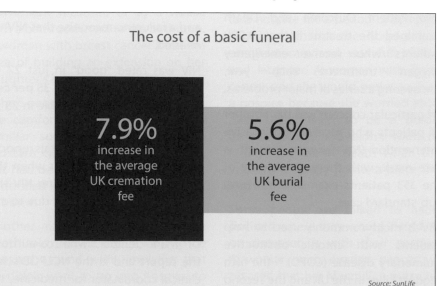

The cost of a basic funeral

7.9% increase in the average UK cremation fee

5.6% increase in the average UK burial fee

Source: SunLife

fee and disbursements, which includes the cremation or burial fee, doctor's fee and clergy/officiate fee.

Funeral director's fees

Funeral director's fees, which usually cover the cost of the coffin, hearse, collection and care of the deceased plus the funeral director's professional guidance, make up the majority of the cost of a basic funeral. This cost has risen, but not by as much as the overall cost of a funeral – it is up 3.3% over the past 12 months from £2,411 to £2,491.

Disbursements

Cremation and burial fees

After the funeral director's fee, the second largest cost is the cremation or burial fee, and the 2017 report shows that both these costs have risen more steeply than the overall cost of a funeral. In 2016, the average UK cremation fee was £733. This has seen the largest increase of all costs – 7.9% to £791 – while the cost of a burial has risen by 5.6% from £1,950 to £2,059.

Funeral directors suggest that councils putting up their prices is the main reason for the steep rise in crematorium costs.

Doctor's fees

This year, doctor's fees for certification has remained unchanged at £164, but are £0 in Scotland.

Minister's fees

The average fee paid for a religious or secular service has increased by 2% from £152 in 2016 to £155.

The difference between burial, cremation and direct cremation costs

In 2017, 25% of funerals were burials, 75% were cremations and of those cremations, 3% were direct cremations. A direct cremation is where the body is cremated immediately after death, without a funeral service.

Burials

Burial costs differ hugely across the UK. The average cost is £4,561, but in London, the average cost is more than half again at £7,311. At the other end of the scale is Northern Ireland, where the cost of a funeral with a burial is £2,895, less than half the cost of one in the capital and 36.5% less than the national average.

Cremations

Cremation costs also differ across the UK, but not as hugely as burial costs. The national average is £3,596, and once again, London has the highest cost at £4,591. However, the South East and South West are not far behind, with cremation funerals in both regions costing more than £4,000 on average.

Direct cremations

For the first time in 2017 we also looked at the growing trend for direct cremations; according to the funeral directors interviewed, one in ten (9.9%) cremations they organised were direct cremations.

The main reason for the rise in popularity is thought to be down to cost; a direct cremation is the most affordable option because there is no service, which not only reduces the costs related to the service itself, but also allows the cremation to take place at less sociable times of the day, which is cheaper.

It is also thought that the fact that some celebrities – including David Bowie in January 2016 – have opted for direct cremations could also have contributed to their rise in popularity.

The average cost of a typical direct cremation in the UK is £1,835, almost half the cost of a standard cremation.

Almost all (94%) of the funeral directors questioned said that they already offer direct cremations and of the ones that don't, a fifth plan to.

Why do funeral costs rise?

Funeral costs are one of the fastest rising costs in the UK, rising 70% in a decade, and 4.7% in just a year, but why?

Burial Costs

£7,311 London
£5,022 East and West Midlands
£4,596 Yorkshire and the Humber
£4,056 Scotland
£4,034 North West
£5,158 South East and East
£4,709 South West
£4,222 North East
£2,895 Northern Ireland
£3,874 Wales

Source: SunLife

Cremation costs

£4,591 London
£3,245 East and West Midlands
£3,774 Yorkshire and the Humber
£3,146 Scotland
£3,142 North West
£4,155 South East and East
£4,117 South West
£3,619 North East
£3,070 Northern Ireland
£3,049 Wales

Source: SunLife

There is no one reason for the rise, as there are several factors which can affect the cost of a funeral, including:

⇨ Cuts to local authority budgets leading to

  • a rise in crematoria costs in order to increase income

  • reduced subsidies for burials.

⇨ Wage increases for

  • local authority staff

  • crematorium staff

  • grave diggers.

⇨ Increases in funeral director fees

⇨ Rising fuel prices

⇨ Mercury emissions abatement targets

⇨ Lack of space for new graves

⇨ Increase in cost of land for burial sites

⇨ Shortage of woodland burial sites

⇨ Increased investment in cemetery infrastructure including road repairs

⇨ Modifications and improvements to crematoriums.

58% of funeral directors think cuts in central government funding is the main reason for the rise in crematoria costs.

2017

⇨ The above information is reprinted with kind permission from SunLife. Please visit www.sunlife.co.uk for further information.

© 2018 SunLife

Interesting funeral facts UK

There are hundreds of ways to honour a life. Funeral ceremonies have been taking place over a range of cultures for thousands of years through many different practices including burial at sea, standard cremation and even sky burials. Some may choose to plan their own funeral entirely, while others are dealt with, planned and arranged by family, loved ones and funeral directors.

An estimated 2.5 billion people watched the funeral of Princess Diana.

But how much do you really know about funerals?

What's the difference between a coffin and a casket?

A casket only has four sides while a coffin has six. Caskets are rectangular in shape and are generally crafted with higher quality material.

Do more people choose a burial or a cremation?

Cremations account for 70% of all funerals in the UK.

This could be for a number of reasons, including reducing the cost of the service, people may just want a simple, no-fuss type funeral and may want to be cremated for the concerns of the environment.

What's the average price of a funeral?

Around £7,622. This includes extras such as catering and flowers. But the average price of a typical funeral service including non-discretionary fees is £3,456.

When was cremation officially made legal?

Cremation was made legal in 1902 after 28 years of campaigning. Cremation usually takes place in a crematorium, but in certain countries, people prefer alternative methods such as open-air cremation.

What is the most ancient evidence of cremation?

In 1969, remains were discovered and estimated to be over 20,000 years old.

Is there a funeral ritual for animals?

Elephants and Chimpanzees are known to bury the dead by throwing leaves and branches on them.

Why are flowers placed on graves of the dead?

Since Roman times, it's thought that the people of Ancient Rome wanted to create a comforting environment for the deceased's spirit. Since then, it is a natural occurrence that people attend funerals and memorial spots with flowers.

What is the average cost for funeral flowers?

£150 is the general cost for memorial service flowers. Funeral flowers are considered a personal tribute to the deceased and are available in a range of styles, colours and sizes.

How many people would like a traditional funeral service for themselves?

27% of people would like a church service with hymns as their send off, while 54% of respondents claimed that they would like a more personal service.

Did you know?

You can hire 'professional mourners' to add to the sad atmosphere of a funeral. The mourners are informed of the deceased and paid to speak to family members as though they were friends.

So, there you have it, a range of funeral facts that you may not have been aware of!

21 September 2016

⇨ The above information is reprinted with kind permission from ISCA Funeral Services Limited. For further information please visit www.iscafunerals.co.uk.

© 2018 ISCA Funeral Services Limited

What we can learn from death rites of the past will help us treat the dead and grieving better today

An article from **The Conversation.**

THE CONVERSATION

By Lindsey Büster, Postdoctoral Researcher, University of Bradford and Jennie Dayes, Counselling Psychologist and Researcher, University of Bradford

These days many people know they are dying long before death finally arrives. Yet death, a natural event, is often seen as a failure of medicine. Despite the additional time modern healthcare may provide us, we still begin our conversations about the wishes of the dying and their families too late – or not at all. This reluctance to accept our own mortality does not serve us well.

This taboo around death is a fairly modern, Western phenomenon. Past and present, societies have dealt with death and dying in diverse ways. It is clear from, for example, the outpouring of grief at Princess Diana's death, and the conversations opening up around the 20th anniversary of the event, that these outlets are needed in our society too. High-profile celebrity deaths serve as sporadic catalysts for conversations that should be happening every day, in everyday lives.

Recent bereavement theory has moved on from thinking of grief as a series of stages, to a continuous process in which the bereaved never fully return to some 'pre-bereaved' status quo. It is increasingly recognised that the living form various sorts of continuing bonds with the dead, as put forward by the sociologist Tony Walter and psychologist Dennis Klass and colleagues – and this is certainly something that can be seen in death practices today across the globe, and among those practised in the past.

In Neolithic Turkey, one funerary rite included the creation of plastered skulls – family members were buried under the floors of their house and after some time the skull was removed and a plaster face lovingly recreated over it. Many of these plastered skulls show evidence of wear and tear, breakage and repair, suggesting that they were used in everyday life, perhaps displayed and passed around among the living. Similarly, in modern-day Indonesia, the dead are kept in houses, fed and brought gifts for many years after death. While in this state they are considered to be ill or asleep – in this case their biological death does not entail social death.

It was not so long ago in the UK that public outpouring of grief and practices that kept the dead close were acceptable. For example, in Victorian England, mourning clothes and jewellery were commonplace – Queen Victoria wore black for decades in mourning for Prince Albert – while keeping tokens such as locks of hair of a deceased loved one were popular.

However, today death has been outsourced to professionals and, for the most part, dying happens in hospitals or hospices. But many doctors and nurses themselves feel uncomfortable with broaching the subject with relatives. Perhaps there are lessons to be drawn from the attitudes of others far removed from us in time and space: the past, and societies on the other side of the globe, are easier to discuss, yet act as prompts to help us discuss more personal experiences.

The Continuing Bonds Project brings together healthcare practitioners and archaeologists at the University of Bradford and LOROS Hospice in Leicester to explore what we can learn from the past, using archaeology to challenge modern perceptions of and attitudes towards death and dying, and as a vehicle through which people can discuss their own mortality and end-of-life care.

Remember, remember

One case study we show our workshop participants is the Holy Right Hand of St Stephen, a relic of the first king of Hungary which has been on display since 1038. Though saints' relics – generally body parts – have been a large part of Christian culture in the past and were not uncommon, they are something many are uncomfortable with today. One workshop participant describes the display of St Stephen's hand as 'selfish', as if he is being exploited beyond the grave. What responsibilities do we have towards the dead? What constitutes 'respect' for them? Archaeology shows us that it is a fluid and culturally embedded concept which differs wildly between societies and individuals.

Memorialisation, through photographs or statues (that served the same purpose in the past), appears to be fundamental to 'respectful' treatment of the dead. Death masks – plaster castings of a dead person's face – and later even photos of the recently departed, were not uncommon as a way to memorialise the dead, even into the 20th century. Yet while taking photographs of the departed in life are celebrated, photographs of dead bodies themselves are less palatable today.

Another example for workshop participants is the statue of the

Egyptian pharaoh Ramesses II, the bust of which resides at the British Museum, while the feet remain in situ at the Ramesseum in Luxor, Egypt. Given that this individual lived in Egypt nearly 3,000 years ago, the statue has kept his memory alive. Yet its fragmented and dispersed nature prompted our participants to wonder how long their loved ones' memories of them would persist after their death, and what legacies they would want to leave.

101 uses for mortal remains

Memorialisation of the dead takes a very different form at the 16th-century Capela dos Ossos in Évora, Portugal, where monks desiring to save the souls of some 5,000 people from overcrowded local cemeteries used their remains to create a chapel of bones. Individual bones were used to create decorative features such as arches and vaulted ceilings.

Workshop participants were unhappy that bones had been removed from their resting place without the permission of the deceased. But for

ow long can our wishes be accommodated after death? The other feature that unsettled them was the dismantling of the skeletons – in the West today, our identity sits firmly with us as individuals, bounded by our physical bodies. Fragmenting our skeletal remains strikes firmly at this sense of identity – and so our sense of social presence. Such scattered remains are nameless, faceless – lacking the very thing that memorials seek to preserve.

In other cultures – and in the past – identity is less individualistic and resonates within larger kin or community groups. Here, distributing bones may be less problematic and a part of the process whereby the recently deceased joins the host of communal ancestors.

Though some of the topics were difficult to discuss, many workshop participants felt they had improved confidence in talking about death, dying and bereavement as a result. The range of practices from the past reminds us of the diverse ways through which death can be negotiated and the extent to which practices that we take

for granted today are in fact culturally embedded, relative and subject to change. Persistent Facebook profiles of dead friends and family to which loved ones post on each anniversary are an example of how traditions are changing.

In a world where death has become increasingly outsourced and medicalised, the diverse ways we treated and remembered our dead in the past should highlight the choices available to us and prompt us to consider those now banned or taboo. At the entrance of the Capela dos Ossos, the monks who built the chapel left an inscription, a momento mori that reminds us: 'We bones that are here, for yours await'.

11 August 2017

⇨ The above information is reprinted with kind permission from *The Conversation*. Please visit www.theconversation.com for further information.

Fascinating funeral and death rituals around the world

No two funerals are the same, and the further you go into different cultures around the world, the more the funeral plans, styles, death rites and rituals change.

lowered and a prayer has been said, the designated mourners dig the soil with heavy spades and cover the coffin, gradually being joined by all mourners taking turns.

prioritise other things they may have to do first; culture critic Lottie Moller saying it is their: 'lack of sentimentality and imagination, and their strong pragmatism'.

Jewish funerals - tearing shirts

With Jewish funerals, the body has to be buried as soon as possible, ideally within 24 hours. Men will usually tear their pristine white shirts to symbolise grief, and have a black ribbon placed on their jacket. Coffins are always closed and always biodegradable, to help the body get as one with nature quicker. Once the coffin has been

Sweden – waiting as long as possible

Conversely, Sweden has a reputation for being in no hurry to bury their loved ones, having the world's longest wait between death and burial – an average of 20 days as of 2016. The law is one month to bury someone, and many Swedes find it is too short. Some Swedish experts have suggested it is because they are practical and

Professional mourners – China and Taiwan

If you feel the sound of those present grieving needs a little assistance, in the Far East it has become common to hire professional mourners, sobbing at will in order to highlight how popular the deceased was and how deeply they will be missed. Not only can they wail convincingly, but after being briefed on the life of the deceased, they are

able to talk with confidence about his/her life, achievements and hobbies to fellow guests. A more extreme way to attract guests to funerals in the East is reputedly to hire strippers to cheer people up. It is said to have originated in Taiwan in 1995, introduced by the local mafia.

New Orleans jazz funerals

The Cajun culture, in New Orleans and Louisiana, blends the solemnity of the European funeral with the more celebratory African tradition, by having a jazz band play slow dirges marching to the funeral, but changing to happier, upbeat music once the funeral is over and the life is celebrated. If you've ever seen *Live And Let Die,* Roger Moore's debut as James Bond, you'd recall the famous opening scene in which a jazz band plays a sad dirge but switches seamlessly into an uptempo jazz tune as an empty coffin is filled with a doomed MI6 agent.

Korean ashes jewellery

In South Korea, an alternative to having ashes handed to you in an urn,

or sprinkled on a hedge, is to have the cremated ashes cleaned, refined and solidified into crystals before being turned into shiny, colourful beads. Not to be worn, these are typically for presentation purposes and displayed in a bottle or a glass container.

Doing funerals differently in the UK

Most funerals in Britain tend to stay close to either a simple religious format, or a non-religious neutral format. Either way, we are used to a solemn, dignified atmosphere with hymns, a hearse carrying a coffin bearing flowers and a religious service, featuring a eulogy, led by a minister inside a chapel of rest.

However, funerals can be creative in their style, format, venue and content. It's not uncommon now to have funerals in Britain where the theme is the deceased's favourite football team, based around their hobbies, or done in the form of letters or even a play. An increasingly popular way to plan your own funeral is to choose the music in advance — whether

it's a hymn, an emotive ballad, or a stomping rock song. According to Alison Crake, president of the National Association of Funeral Directors, popular music is 'certainly becoming more commonplace' at funerals.

Plan ahead for how you want your funeral to be

It's getting more common nowadays to want to have a say in your send-off, and personalise your own funeral while keeping it respectful. It could be the colour of the clothes you want people to wear, the type of funeral service (e.g. civil, religious or otherwise), the music that's played, or how you'd wish your family and friends to be involved.

14 August 2017

⇨ The above information is reprinted with kind permission from *The Telegraph*. Please visit www.telegraph.co.uk for further information.

Tears in heaven: ten inspirational modern funeral songs

Songs about love and loss can seem even more significant when they are played at a funeral – and even more so, when the song in question was written in tribute to someone who died.

While funeral hymns and sombre music are traditional, the songs we loved in our happiest moments are becoming the memorial songs of choice at many final farewells today.

These ten hits from the 80s, 90s, Noughties and more recent years have become evergreen funeral songs. With lyrics written in loving memory, they are modern funeral songs with incredible meaning.

1. When September Ends – Green Day

'As my memory rests, but never forgets what I lost.'

Green Day frontman Billie Joe Armstrong was just ten years old when his father, Andrew, died of cancer.

This evergreen classic is a fitting modern funeral song, which Billie Joe has described as therapeutic to write, but sometimes difficult to perform due to the emotions behind the poignant lyrics.

2. Tears in Heaven – Eric Clapton

'Would you know my name, if I saw you in Heaven?'

Eric Clapton channelled his grief following the heartbreaking death of his four-year-old son, Conor, into the lyrics of this timeless funeral song.

When you are lost for words and grieving, it is among the modern funeral songs that expresses in words and music what is almost impossible to say.

3. Keep Me in Your Heart – Warren Zevon

'If I leave you, it doesn't mean I love you any less.'

Rocker Warren Zevon penned this heartbreaking goodbye after he was diagnosed with terminal cancer that took his life a year later.

If you are searching for funeral songs with meaning, this song is worth a listen if you are unfamiliar with it. Indeed, many of the tracks that feature on Zevon's final album, The Wind, are worthy modern funeral songs, with reflections upon life, death and the people left behind.

4. The Show Must Go On – Queen

'I can fly, my friends.'

A terminally ill Freddie Mercury was becoming frail when he came to record The Show Must Go On, but his incredible voice was as strong as ever, as Queen recorded their final studio album together.

Expressing courage in the face of final days that came way too soon, it's a deeply moving and uplifting funeral anthem for rockers who turned it up to 11.

5. Go Rest High on That Mountain – Vince Gill

'Son, your work on Earth is done.'

Bittersweet country numbers often touch a chord deep in our hearts and make touching songs for funerals.

This song has been amongst the most popular funeral songs since country star Vince Gill released it in 1994. He began writing it in tribute to another country star, Keith Whitely, but it was the death of Vince's brother, Bob, that moved him to finish the song, in memory of them both.

6. I'll Be Missing You – Puff Daddy and Faith Evans

'Can't believe you ain't here.'

Shortly after the murder of his good friend, rapper Notorious B.I.G., rap star Puff Daddy wrote, recorded and released this Billboard chart-busting tribute. It has been one of modern funeral music's most-played songs ever since.

The beat was sampled from The Police hit Every Breath You Take, while the song also features extracts from composer Samuel Barber's Adagio for Strings, which was amongst the funeral music played for President John F. Kennedy, Albert Einstein and Princess Grace of Monaco.

7. The Living Years – Mike and the Mechanics

'I just wish I could have told him, in the living years.'

Singer B.A. Robertson and musician Mike Rutherford had both lost their fathers when they co-wrote this poignant modern funeral song and tied their experiences into the lyrics.

Rutherford has said that he's had hundreds of letters from fans saying it's helped them pick up the phone following an estrangement. For others, it's a memorial song which brings a lump to the throat and evokes what they felt in their heart for their dad.

8. Meet Me in the Middle of the Air – Paul Kelly

'Fear not death's dark shadow, I will meet you in the middle of the air.'

Legendary Aussie singer-songwriter Paul Kelly and guitarist Charlie Owen released an entire album of funeral songs, Death's Dateless Night, in 2016.

Inspired to record it after attending the funeral of a friend, it includes arrangements of evergreen classics such as The Parting Glass and arrangements of some of Kelly's own best-known songs, including Meet Me in the Middle of the Air. He revealed the tracks are the most popular funeral songs he's requested to play at people's final send-offs.

9. See You Again – Wiz Khalifa

'Everything that I went through, you were standing there by my side.'

This was written in memory of film star Paul Walker and featured on the soundtrack of the movie *Furious 7*.

It was the world's biggest selling song in 2015 and its touching lyrics also struck a chord with people remembering their own loved ones. It has already become one of the most popular modern songs for funerals and memorial services.

10. Courtney's Song – James Blunt

'There's still your name on my phone, I can't believe I'm not able to call.'

James Blunt wrote this beautiful memorial song in tribute to his good friend, actress Carrie Fisher and her mother Debbie Reynolds, who died just a day apart in 2016.

It was played at their joint public memorial in March this year and is likely to become a poignant funeral song in the years to come. Debbie's son Todd Fisher said: "Everybody has lost somebody and this song is a true help in letting go."

6 September 2017

⇨ The above information is reprinted with kind permission from Funeral Zone. Please visit www.funeralzone.co.uk for further information.

20 of the coolest funeral ideas to celebrate life

As well as the chance to say goodbye to a loved one, a funeral is also the perfect occasion to celebrate their life. There are so many ways this can be done, so we have compiled our top 20 suggestions to provide some inspiration and some really unique ideas.

1. A message book

A message book can be the perfect addition to a funeral service or wake to help memorialise people's fond memories of the deceased. Simply ask friends and family members to write down a memory about the deceased that makes them smile. The book can then be shared with loved ones after the funeral and can be an incredible comfort as well as a great way to celebrate many of the happiest moments in someone's life.

2. Tree planting

By planting a tree as part of a funeral service, mourners are able to witness something that will continue to live, grow and thrive in memory of the deceased. This can also become a comforting place to visit for close friends and family. By adding a plaque to the tree, others can take a moment to appreciate the tree as a celebration of someone's life too.

3. Fundraising

If the deceased was passionate about a particular charity or cause, then why not include a fundraising element to their funeral? The funds raised can make a difference to a charity of their choice and that in itself is a great way to celebrate life and highlight the kindness of the person who has been laid to rest.

4. Photo collage

Ask those attending the funeral to bring along any photographs they would like to be included in a photo collage or photograph album celebrating the deceased's life in images. This can be a great reason to connect with friends and family again after the funeral to share the end result.

5. Celebrate life in full colour

Many people are opting to avoid the tradition of mourners wearing black to a funeral and asking those attending to wear bright and colourful clothes instead. This is a great way to celebrate life in full colour!

6. Pick a colour

Another great way to brighten up the funeral congregation and remember the deceased fondly is to ask mourners to wear something in the deceased's favourite colour. This could be connected to a sports team, hobby or just because they liked a particular colour. It could be just one item of clothing, maybe a tie or a scarf, or an entire outfit.

7. Photo slide show

A beautiful way to celebrate someone's life is to create a slide show of photos that can be shown at the funeral or wake. Pictures are a great way to highlight memorable times in someone's life and a slide show is the perfect way to share these with others. A favourite song or piece of music can be played at the same time too.

8. Forget me not

Flowers can be a beautiful way to remember someone, so why not hand out 'forget me not' seeds to mourners to take home and plant as a fitting way to remember the person who has been laid to rest?

9. Memory table

To really highlight the achievements in someone's life, why not display a memory table during the service or wake? This could include pictures, trophies, favourite items of clothing, a favourite mug or anything that people will fondly associate with the deceased or be interested to see.

10. Worldly wise

For a well-travelled loved one or someone who simply loved to explore, you could display a world map showing all the places they visited in their lifetime. This is something that can be displayed on the day of the funeral but also displayed afterwards to extend the celebration of life. It can be a great prompt to talk about the deceased and keep their memory alive.

11. Light up life

Memorial candles are another great gift to give to friends and family enabling them to enjoy moments where they think of the deceased. Candle lids or labels can contain a message or simply the deceased name, birth and death dates, but when lit you can be sure they will be thought of.

12. Themed funerals

For those who really want something a bit different to celebrate someone's life then themed funerals are on the increase. From superheroes to Christmas, or sport to musical themes,

this is a great way to allow people to enjoy a fun yet fitting send off, celebrating the deceased's life and wishes.

13. Music matters

Music can be an apt way to celebrate someone's life and bring back many memories to those attending the funeral. The music played during the funeral and also at the wake is a fitting way to celebrate someone's life. You could consider a tribute act covering one of their favourite singers or groups, or compiling a playlist of their favourite songs. Maybe even a gospel choir or jazz band! If they loved to dance, then encourage mourners to feel free to dance in their memory.

14. Going out with a bang

Fireworks add something special to any occasion, so why not a funeral? A firework display can provide a stunning and exciting end to a funeral service, celebrating someone's life in full colour and with a bang!

15. Message in a bottle

To celebrate life and send the memory of the deceased on one last adventure,

why not write about them and place your message and contact details in a bottle. Set the bottle off on its travels at a favourite coastal spot and you never know, someone may get in touch from far away to say that your message reached them. What a lovely way to remember your loved one.

16. Transport

The choice of transport used as part of the funeral ceremony can also be a fitting way to remember a loved one and celebrate their life. There are many choices available now from a tractor and trailer to a horse and cart, or a motorbike with a sidecar and even a campervan. If your loved one was enthusiastic about a specific type of vehicle or maybe they were a bus driver or lorry driver, then don't overlook the mode of funeral transport as a way to provide a great sendoff.

17. Take flight

Setting off balloons in memory of a loved one provides a beautiful experience for friends and family. Messages can even be attached to the balloons as a touching way to say a final farewell as loved ones watch their messages take flight.

18. A breath of fresh air

To remember someone who loved nature or the outdoors then an outdoor funeral service or wake can be a great way to celebrate something they loved and appreciated in life. Of course Mother Nature may impact this idea, but weather permitting an outdoor service or sendoff can be therapeutic and comforting.

19. Open mic

When there are many mourners at a funeral it is often difficult to spend time and share memories with everyone. By offering an open mic session, those who would like to say a few words or share a particular memory can do so with everyone. Friends and family members may learn things about their loved one that they didn't know or hear stories for the first time. This is a fun and friendly way to share and bring mourners together.

20. Personalised coffin

Not surprisingly we wholeheartedly love the way that a personalised coffin can memorialise a person and be used to celebrate their life. With endless design options, including completely personalised designs or photographic designs, a personalised coffin provides the perfect pictorial tribute. With the coffin often being the focal point of the funeral service, it is the perfect chance to display something that the deceased loved in a fitting design.

29 June 2017

⇨ The above information is reprinted with kind permission from Greenfield Coffins. Please visit www.greenfieldcoffins.co.uk for further information.

Where can you scatter ashes?

Where can you scatter ashes? There is a lot to think about, so here are some pointers. Once you have considered the location you will need permission.

Private land – Private and secluded, you will have your own space and time. Make sure you have permission, make sure returning will be easy. For example a golf course is a popular choice, but revisiting the site may be awkward if none of your friends or relatives are members.

Beauty spots – There has been problems with excessive use of beauty spots and it is unlikely you will get any privacy. Arranging a ceremony on a busy day, at a much visited site could lead to problems with other visitors enjoying the site.

Rivers – It is acceptable – says the Environment Agency – but don't put anything in the river that will not degrade, e.g. plastics.

At sea – You can opt to use a boat or scatter on the shoreline or beach.

Mountain or hill tops – Can be a dramatic and inspiring setting but there are a few reasons why you should perhaps reconsider spreading ashes at the very summit:

⇨ you can't predict where the ashes may blow and it can be very upsetting to those present if they end up being caught by a squally gust

⇨ it could be busy

⇨ cremation ashes can have serious impact on the local environment. Plant species found in such places are very sensitive – human ashes contain a lot of phosphate that will upset the local habit.

⇨ you should consider somewhere off the beaten track, not at the very top perhaps around a tree, cairn or lake on the ascent.

In a wood or tree planting site – You can choose to plant one anywhere you get permission, but you will be responsible for it. You could consider a tree in a memorial wood.

Common land: It is best not assume that if land is 'common land' like a village green, that you are entitled scatter your ashes there. Common land usually means you have the right do certain things there, e.g. to walk over it or even graze sheep.

Sports venues: Often a popular choice if the deceased had a particular sporting passion, football pitches, golf courses, cricket pitches, rugby stadium, and horse racing courses. Permission for scattering funeral ashes at private sports facilities is dependant on the policy of the individual club. You will need to approach the ground's owner, and a word of warning – if the venue is private, as with many golf clubs – revisiting the site may prove awkward.

⇨ The above information is reprinted with kind permission from Scattering Ashes. Please visit www.scattering-ashes.co.uk for further information.

Bereavement

Coping with bereavement

The death of a loved one can be devastating. Bereavement counsellor Sarah Smith describes some of the feelings that can arise from losing someone, and where you can go for help and support.

Bereavement affects people in different ways. There's no right or wrong way to feel.

'You might feel a lot of emotions at once, or feel you're having a good day, then you wake up and feel worse again,' says Sarah, who works at Trinity Hospice in London.

She says powerful feelings can come unexpectedly. 'It's like waves on a beach. You can be standing in water up to your knees and feel you can cope, then suddenly a big wave comes and knocks you off your feet.'

Stages of bereavement or grief

Experts generally accept there are four stages of bereavement:

⇨ accepting that your loss is real

⇨ experiencing the pain of grief

⇨ adjusting to life without the person who has died

⇨ putting less emotional energy into grieving and putting it into something new – in other words, moving on.

You'll probably go through all these stages, but you won't necessarily move smoothly from one to the next. Your grief might feel chaotic and out of control, but these feelings will eventually become less intense.

Feelings of grief

Give yourself time – these feelings will pass. You might feel:

⇨ shock and numbness – this is usually the first reaction to the death, and people often speak of being in a daze

⇨ overwhelming sadness, with lots of crying

⇨ tiredness or exhaustion

⇨ anger – for example, towards the person who died, their illness, or God

⇨ guilt – for example, guilt about feeling angry, about something you said or didn't say, or about not being able to stop your loved one dying.

'These feelings are all perfectly normal,' says Sarah. 'The negative feelings don't make you a bad person. Lots of people feel guilty about their anger, but it's OK to be angry and to question why.'

She adds some people become forgetful and less able to concentrate. You might lose things, such as your keys. This is because your mind is distracted by bereavement and grief, says Sarah. You're not losing your sanity.

The GOV.UK website has information on what to do after someone dies,

such as registering the death and planning a funeral.

Coping with grief

Talking and sharing your feelings with someone can help. Don't go through this alone. For some people, relying on family and friends is the best way to cope.

If you don't feel you can talk to them much – perhaps you aren't close, or they're grieving, too – you can contact local bereavement services through:

⇨ your local hospice

⇨ the national Cruse helpline on 0808 808 1677

⇨ your GP.

A bereavement counsellor can give you time and space to talk about your feelings, including the person who has died, your relationship, family, work, fears and the future.

You can have access to a bereavement counsellor at any time, even if the person you lost died a long time ago.

Talking about the person who has died

Don't be afraid to talk about the person who has died. People in your life might not mention their name because they

STAGES OF BEREAVEMENT OR GRIEF

Accepting that your loss is real...

Experiencing the pain of grief...

Adjusting to life without the person who died...

Putting less emotional energy into grieving and putting it into something new – in other words, moving on.

don't want to upset you. But if you feel you can't talk to them, it can make you feel isolated.

Anniversaries and special occasions can be hard. Sarah suggests doing whatever you need to do to get through the day. This might be taking a day off work or doing something that reminds you of that person, such as taking a favourite walk.

If you need help to move on

Each bereavement is unique, and you can't tell how long it will last. 'In general, the death and the person might not constantly be at the forefront of your mind after around 18 months,' says Sarah. This period may be shorter or longer for some people, which is normal.

Your GP or a bereavement counsellor can help if you feel you're not coping. Some people also get support from a religious minister.

You might need help if:

⇨ you can't get out of bed

⇨ you neglect yourself or your family – for example, you don't eat properly

⇨ you feel you can't go on without the person you've lost

⇨ the emotion is so intense it's affecting the rest of your life – for example, you can't face going to work or you're taking your anger out on someone else.

These feelings are normal – as long as they don't last for a long time. 'The time to get help depends on the person,' says Sarah.

'If these things last for a period that you feel is too long or your family say they're worried, that's the time to seek help. Your GP can refer you, and they can monitor your general health.'

Some people turn to alcohol or drugs during difficult times. Get help cutting down on alcohol, or see the Frank website for information on drugs.

Counselling if someone is dying

If someone has an incurable illness, they and their loved ones can prepare for bereavement.

'Practical things can help, such as discussing funeral arrangements together and making a will,' says Sarah.

Bereavement counsellors also offer pre-bereavement care, helping patients and their family cope with their feelings.

This can be especially important for children, Sarah explains. 'Children's stress levels are at their highest before their family member dies, so support during this time is important.'

28 February 2017

⇨ The above information is reproduced with kind permission from the NHS. Please visit www.nhs.uk for further information.

How the internet is changing the way we grieve

An article from The Conversation.

THE CONVERSATION

By Jo Bell, Senior Lecturer, Faculty of Health Sciences, University of Hull

People don't die in the same way that they used to. In the past, a relative, friend, partner would pass away, and in time, all that would be left would be memories and a collection of photographs. These days the dead are now forever present online and digital encounters with someone who has passed away are becoming a common experience.

Each one of us has a digital footprint – the accumulation of our online activity that chronicles a life lived online through blogs, pictures, games, websites, networks, shared stories and experiences.

When a person dies, their 'virtual selves' remain out there for people to see and interact with. These virtual selves exist in the same online spaces that many people use every day. And this is a new and unfamiliar phenomenon that some people might find troubling – previously dead people were not present in this way.

Yet for some, these spaces have become a valuable tool – especially so for the bereaved. An emerging body of research is now looking at the ways the Internet, including social media and memorial websites, are enabling new ways of grieving – that transcend traditional notions of 'letting go' and 'moving on'.

Forever online

A colleague and I first got interested in how deceased loved ones were being remembered online a few years ago. My particular interest at the time was in how suicides were being memorialised online and what motivated people to do this. I also wanted to know how these online memorials impacted people's grief and the trauma of being bereaved by suicide – as well as how these online spaces changed over time.

Turning to social media for support when dealing with bereavement and the loss of a loved one helps mourners and others make sense of a death by talking about it. This helps to make it a much less isolating experience. It provides the bereaved with a 'community of mourners', or as one of our participants put it:

'I've got 67 people in my life who I can share my grief with... and they all understand where I'm coming from.'

For many mourners, the most important motivating factor seems to be the need to stay connected to the deceased and to 'keep them alive'. And keeping a Facebook page going by actively maintaining the 'in life' profile of the deceased, or creating a new 'in memorial' profile, allows users to send private or public messages to the deceased and to publicly express their grief. In our research, accounts of talking to the deceased on Facebook were common:

'People go up [to his Facebook site] and put mementos on and they'll say on Facebook, been to see you today Mark... yesterday I went up and I just chatted to him...

'Now more than three-and-a-half years on... they write and say really miss you Mark or I'm doing this and it reminded

me of you… he's still being included in what his friends are doing.'

The use of social media in this way goes some way towards answering the question of where to put one's feelings – such as love, grief, guilt – after a death. And many people turn to the same sites to promote awareness raising and fundraising for various charities in memory of their loved ones.

Virtual living

In this sense then, keeping the deceased alive on Facebook is a way of working against loss. It illustrates how social networking sites are replacing traditional mourning objects – such as items of jewellery, clothing or gravestones – that are imbued with particular emotional resonance and which subsequently take on additional significance after the death.

Unlike sentimental objects, social media pages and online spaces allow people to explore grief with others from the comfort of their own home. Talking to people online can also help to free up some of the inhibitions that are otherwise felt when talking about loss – it enables forms of uncensored self-expression that are not comparable with face-to-face conversations.

So although the physical bond to a loved one may be gone, a virtual presence remains and evolves after death. And in this way, online memorial sites and social networking spaces help the bereaved to see how events in the past can continue to have value and meaning in the present and the future.

31 July 2018

⇨ The above information is reprinted with kind permission from *The Conversation*. Please visit www.theconversation.com for further information.

How do you deal with grief – fall apart under its weight, or stay strong?

Since my sister's suicide I have gone on – for her son, for my kids, for me. The sadness will stay but I am bigger than my grief.

By Lea Walters

One year ago to this day, my sister died by suicide.

The phone rang. I heard the words as if from a distance. My heart caved in, my mind froze, my body disappeared. I pulled myself together enough to call my nephew – a shattered young man – before I completely broke down.

Two days later, I was on national TV, launching my long-awaited book on strength-based parenting. Three months later, I was in Montreal accepting the presidency of the International Positive Psychology Association.

Just as many of my dreams were coming true, my world was falling apart. I was confronted head-on with the irony of reaching a professional zenith in the field of positive psychology at exactly the same time I was dealing with excruciating personal darkness and loss. How would my expertise deal with this king hit?

My sister was proud of my book. She read various sections and loved it. We both shared a passion for helping others. I'd written this acknowledgment to her:

To my beautiful sister, Colleen, an amazing social worker who has used her strengths of courage, persistence and compassion to help thousands of people… You have made such a positive difference to the world.

I'd been saving it to show her in person. She never saw it.

The night after she died I was so incapacitated by grief that my husband's mother and sister had to help me pack for the book tour: 'You need a suit for TV… this skirt… these shoes… where's your passport?' In interviews, I'd smile and discuss how to create happy families. Then I'd crawl into bed and weep. PTSD flashbacks from my childhood would stop me from sleeping.

I expected the emotional pain but was taken aback by the physical pain. For months, sharp pain radiated down my face, through my throat and across my ribcage. Painkillers did nothing. Friends were shocked when I'd double over in mid-sentence.

Colleen and I didn't have a perfect relationship. Growing up with abuse strained our bond. But we loved and understood each other. We were bridesmaids at each other's weddings and the first person we called when we each found out we were pregnant. We supported each other to seek therapy. No matter what, we knew we were there for each other. We were survivors. But now I am left without her and I have no words to describe the pain.

My friends worried that I wasn't addressing my grief. Some advised cancelling my tour. To be honest, I couldn't tell if the tour was a good thing because it kept me together, or a bad thing because it stopped me from falling apart.

Fall apart. That's what you're supposed to do when a loved one dies, right? Or are you supposed to stay strong? Is it OK to be happy? Is it selfish to go on?

Life doesn't pause to help us answer these questions. Each of us must find our own answers as we go.

If I had to sum it up, I'd say: allow yourself to fall apart in some moments AND will yourself to stay strong in others.

I didn't do this perfectly, but here are some ways that I navigated as best I could:

Use mindfulness to be present to your feelings and needs

Mindfulness helped me feel the loss and deal with the PTSD flashbacks but not be overwhelmed. I tried to be present to all of the feelings moving through me, knowing I was bigger than the grief; that I could let it wash over me but that I'd come back.

Understand that others will respond based on their relationship with death

Try not to take it personally. Some friends sat with me in the messiness of it all. Others dropped away for months, later confiding: "I just didn't know what to say." Many people are afraid of suicide and don't have a language to talk about it. But I decided to talk about it and about her. The way my sister died does not define her. The 44 years she spent on this Earth – helping others as a social worker and raising a good son – these define her.

Draw on your strengths to comfort and steady you.

Each of us has our own unique strengths. Grief amplifies the need for us to use them. For me, Colleen's death was a call to action to step more fully into my nephew's life and to use my strengths as a psychologist to help him through his profound loss. I couldn't be more proud of my nephew and the strength he has shown over this past year – wisdom, dignity, compassion and grit beyond his years.

Seek healing, more than happiness

People advised me to try and stay happy. That wasn't working for me, yet I didn't want to drown in grief. I had my nephew and my kids to look after, not to mention the book tour. I decided to focus on 'healing' rather than 'happiness,' engaging in healing practices like journaling, walking, prayer, and meditation.

Hold on to the small moments of light.

To ensure that I didn't drown in sadness, I made a choice to savour the good things: the immense gratitude I felt for my husband, his family and my loving friends (I had a freezer full of casseroles for 6 months); life's little joys – sunshine on my back, the smell of good coffee, my kids' laughter and the affection of my dog who, for months after Colleen died, followed me around the house gently nudging my leg with his nose. These small things made the grief less daunting.

Give yourself permission to walk away.

Grieving is warrior work. It takes enormous amounts of energy. Do you need time by yourself? Take it. Are there things you can take off your plate? Do so. Are there people in your life who are unsupportive, or outright harmful? Walk away. It may not be forever, but you need to protect yourself during this time.

Be authentic and courageous.

'Putting on a brave face must take so much out of you,' one friend commented after a book event. But bravery was not a face I put on to hide my grief. Bravery was born because of the grief. I had to have the courage to talk about her death in order to honour her and support her son. When all I wanted to do was crawl into a ball, I willed myself to speak up about suicide and abuse in the hope that it will help others who are going through similar circumstances. You will have your own circumstances but I encourage you to be real and courageous.

I miss Coll every day. I keep expecting a text from her with a funny joke or the lyric from an eighties' song. I keep going to dial her to tell her the latest gossip. I haven't 'moved on'. But I have 'gone on'. I don't ever want to move on from my sister, she is a part of me and I always want her in my life. But I know I need to go on for the sake of her son, my kids and myself. The raw grief still hits me at unexpected moments – like a sudden punch to the throat – but it's happening less frequently. Most days the rawness has been replaced by a soft sadness. I know that this sadness will be with me for the rest of my life but, as time passes, I find myself thinking of our fun times and my body warms. With each happy memory of my darling sister, the warmth will grow. I know that the warmth won't replace the sadness but I trust that they will find a way to sit beside each other.

I feel Colleen is somewhere cheering my work. Her work was about rescuing kids from unhappy families and mine is about helping kids thrive by creating happy families. Her legacy lives on through my book.

Embracing life doesn't mean denying a loved one's death, or that we miss them less. It means honouring and celebrating their life. It means taking over where they left off. But most of all, it means having our eyes open to the enormous gifts we gain in our own life as we continue to stumble and get back up again.

26 May 2018

⇨ The above information is reprinted with kind permission from *The Guardian*. Please visit www.theguardian.com for further information.

'Broken heart syndrome' can cause long-lasting damage to health, study reveals

Symptoms are similar to a heart attack.

By Brogan Driscoll, Lifestyle Editor

'Broken heart syndrome' – which can be triggered by severe emotional distress, such as the death of a loved one – may leave longer lasting damage than previously thought, experts have revealed.

Around 3,000 people per year in the UK suffer from the condition, also known as Takotsubo syndrome, according to the Press Association.

Symptoms are similar to a heart attack and the condition, which mostly affects women, is usually diagnosed in hospital.

Until now, it was thought the heart fully recovered from the syndrome, but new research suggests the muscle actually suffers long-term damage.

This could explain why people with the syndrome only tend to have the same life expectancy as those who suffer a heart attack.

The research, funded by the British Heart Foundation (BHF), was published in the *Journal of the American Society of Echocardiography*.

A team from the University of Aberdeen followed 52 Takotsubo patients over the course of four months.

They used ultrasound and cardiac MRI scans to look at how the patients' hearts were functioning.

The results showed that the syndrome permanently affected the heart's pumping motion, delaying the twisting or 'wringing' motion made by the heart during a heartbeat.

The heart's squeezing motion was also reduced, while parts of the heart muscle suffered scarring, which affected the elasticity of the heart and prevented it from contracting properly. Dr Dana Dawson, reader in cardiovascular medicine at the University of Aberdeen, who led the research, said: 'We used to think that people who suffered from Takotsubo cardiomyopathy would fully recover, without medical intervention.

'Here we've shown that this disease has much longer lasting damaging effects on the hearts of those who suffer from it.'

Figures show that between 3% and 17% of people with the syndrome die within five years of diagnosis.

Some 90% of sufferers are female and a stressful trigger is identified in around 70% of cases.

Professor Metin Avkiran, associate medical director at the BHF, said: 'This study has shown that in some patients who develop Takotsubo syndrome various aspects of heart function remain abnormal for up to four months afterwards.

'Worryingly, these patients' hearts appear to show a form of scarring, indicating that full recovery may take much longer, or indeed may not occur, with current care.

'This highlights the need to urgently find new and more effective treatments for this devastating condition.'

19 June 2017

⇨ The above information is reprinted with kind permission from The Huffington Post UK. Please visit www.huffingtonpost.co.uk for further information.

Is it OK to take a young child to a funeral?

By Rachel Halliwell

Seeing the distress on her ten-year-old daughter Charlotte's face as her mother-in-law's coffin was carried into church, Katherine Nicholson instantly regretted allowing her child to attend a funeral so young. 'She was distraught,' says Katherine. 'She couldn't take her eyes off the coffin and was sobbing as she gripped my hand.

'Charlotte's weeping continued throughout the service, but when I offered to step outside with her she smiled, shook her head, and insisted she wanted to stay.'

Charlotte and her grandmother, who died last year aged 84, were extremely close. But when funeral arrangements were discussed, Katherine, a publisher from Ipswich, presumed her daughter wouldn't attend. She says: 'I thought ten was too young to be exposed to the grief of a funeral. They're emotionally draining, and the idea of my child experiencing something so harrowing seemed cruel.

'Her grandmother dying was her first experience of death. I thought that was enough for her to have to deal with at that age.'

But Charlotte, and Katherine's husband, Nick, a college lecturer, were adamant she should attend. 'Charlotte wanted to say a proper goodbye, and Nick felt it wrong to skirt around the fact that death and the rituals surrounding it are a part of life,' says Katherine.

'As she became increasingly distraught at the idea of being somewhere else while we were at the funeral, I started to think that perhaps she really did need to be there with us so that she could feel a part of it all.'

Deciding whether it is appropriate for a child at primary school to attend a family funeral is something parents are unlikely to consider until they have to.

According to a British Social Attitudes survey, almost half of people (48 per cent) think that children under 12 should attend funerals, while just over a quarter (26 per cent) believe they should be kept away. The remainder say the child's maturity and relationship would be deciding factors.

It's a dilemma, and one that crops up regularly on a helpline run by the childhood bereavement charity, Winston's Wish.

'There's understandable anxiety, especially when there are conflicting opinions between family members on what's the right thing to do,' says Di Stubbs, a child bereavement expert with 20 years' experience, who works on the helpline. 'We can't give people the answer – this is their family and everyone's situation is personal to them. But what we can do is speak as outsiders and share, through our many years of experience, the child's perspective on this.'

Of great significance, says Di, is that, of the thousands of children Winston's Wish has supported through bereavement since its inception 25 years ago, none have ever said after the funeral of a loved one that they regretted attending.

But she adds: 'We've spoken to hundreds of children who didn't go and they say they do regret that. Funerals are desperately sad occasions, but sadness isn't something children need to be protected from – it's a very natural part of grief.'

Dr Katie Koehler, child psychologist and deputy director of Bereavement Support and Education for Child Bereavement UK, points out that most adults gain comfort from the opportunity to say goodbye at a funeral, and that this is no different for children.

'However, it is important that they are given the choice to be there or not, and are well prepared for what to expect,' she says.

'A very young child, toddler, or even a baby can be there with the rest of the family. Although they may not understand at the time, when they grow older children appreciate

knowing that, along with everyone else, they were a part of this important event.'

Our 11-year-old daughter, Bridie, recently attended the funeral of her great-aunt, who died aged 91. This was someone we loved, and who had lived a long and interesting life; we knew the occasion would be desperately sad, but also an opportunity to celebrate a life lived well. Both my husband and I thought our daughter should be a part of that. In preparation, beforehand we showed her pictures of the crematorium where the service would be held, and explained the rituals that would take place.

'It's also important to prepare your child for the fact that lots of people around them will be dreadfully upset,' says Di. 'Tell them, 'yes, I will be crying my heart out, because I will be so desperately sad'. But also let them know that you will still be around for cuddles, and even play a game together before bed.

'We have this terrible protection racket going on with children when we decide to hide our feelings during times of grief. But actually, they need to know that adults can feel huge things and yet somehow still be able to get up and carry on. By seeing that Mummy got upset after Granny's funeral, but was still able to blow her nose and go to the shop for milk, they will understand that you can withstand death.'

After her grandmother's funeral Charlotte insisted she was glad she went. 'She said it was sad but not at all frightening,' says Katherine. 'She enjoyed hearing people talking about her grandmother, both during the service and afterwards, and enjoyed hearing stories about her life that were new to her.' Our daughter expressed similar sentiments.

But while their experiences were positive, Di says it's important for children to know it's OK not to go – and that there are alternatives.

'If there are family tensions or complications, you can still do something special to remember a loved one, and perhaps get someone who attended to bring back a service sheet, so your child has something real to hold on to.

'And if someone thinks, 'Oh no, I didn't let her go to her granny's funeral and now I wish I had', you can hold a memorial service or gather somewhere that was special to the person who died and remember them together.'

Preparing a child for the service

Funerals can be confusing for a child, and it helps to warn them that people won't just be tearful on the day – there is likely to be smiling as people greet old friends and relatives they might not have seen for a long time.

Children often worry about what will happen to the body after a funeral. Therapists use a technique where they get the child to do things with a gloved hand such as pick up toys or open a window. They then take the glove off and talk about how it now can't do any of those things and explain that's a bit like Grandma's body now. To put the glove in the ground won't hurt the glove, and it won't hurt Grandma, either.

Don't be afraid of the fact that your child is likely to be very upset on the day. Di Stubbs adds: 'Explain that these are upsetting occasions and that at a funeral it really is OK to feel as sad as sad can be, and they'll be far from alone in feeling that way.'

7 October 2017

⇨ The above information is reprinted with kind permission from *The Telegraph*. Please visit www.telegraph.co.uk for further information.

Sensing the dead is perfectly normal – and often helpful

An article from The Conversation.

THE CONVERSATION

By Simon McCarthy-Jones, Associate Professor in Clinical Psychology and Neuropsycology, Trinity College, Dublin

Céline Dion recently revealed that she still senses the presence of her husband, even though he died from cancer in January 2016. What's more, the Canadian singer said she still talks to René Angélil, who she was married to for 22 years, and can still hear him at times.

While her remarks prompted ridicule in some quarters, seeing, hearing or sensing the presence of a deceased loved one is nothing to be ashamed of. On the contrary, it is a perfectly normal and often helpful way of dealing with grief.

Sensing a deceased spouse is remarkably common. Between 30 and 60% of elderly widowed people experience so-called bereavement hallucinations. In his book, *Hallucinations*, the late neurologist Oliver Sacks gives the following example. Marion, who had lost her husband, Paul, came home from work one day:

'Usually at that hour Paul would have been at his electronic chessboard … His table was out of sight… but he greeted me in his familiar way 'Hello! You're back! Hi!' His voice was clear and strong and true… the speech was live and real.'

This is not rare. A study of elderly widows and widowers in Wales found that 13% had heard their dead loved one's voice, 14% had seen them and 3% had felt their touch. By far the greatest number, 39%, said they continued to feel the presence of loved ones.

Such experiences can encourage people to talk to their lost loved one, which the study found 12% did. This talking can be accompanied by a feeling that the dead spouse is listening.

Intriguingly, it has been found that those who talk to their dead spouse are more likely to be coping with widowhood than those who don't.

It doesn't have to be a partner or spouse who dies. For example, a study of bereavement hallucinations in people of a range of ages described the experiences of Samuel, who had lost his grandmother. One day, when trying to work out where the problem was with a waste disposal unit, he heard her say, 'It's at the back. It's at the back.' And so it was.

Grateful for the dead

Multiple studies have found that more than two thirds of the widowed find their hallucinations pleasant or helpful. The experiences can provide spiritual and emotional strength and comfort, reduce feelings of isolation and give people encouragement during difficult tasks.

Take the experience of Aggie, which she recounted to researchers as part of a study of bereavement hallucinations. Her boyfriend knew he was dying but hid it, ending their relationship to try to spare her pain. After he died,

Aggie heard his voice apologising for pushing her away at the end. She had partly blamed herself for his death and felt guilty. Hearing his voice helped Aggie to forgive herself.

Such experiences will typically fade over time.

The dark side

Of course, bereavement hallucinations can be problematic. When they first happen, some people will get very upset when they realise that the deceased person has not actually returned. The hallucination can also be traumatising. A woman who lost her daughter to a heroin overdose reported hearing her voice crying out, 'Mamma, Mamma!… It's so cold.' In the widowed, they can prevent new relationships developing.

Also, death does not become everyone. After her mother died, Julie started hearing her voice. It called her a slag, slut and whore. It told her she wasn't fit to live and encouraged her to overdose on pills. Julie's relationship with her mother had been problematic, but she'd never said such things while alive.

Thankfully, negative experiences are rare. One study reported that only 6% of people found bereavement hallucinations unpleasant. These experiences hardly ever require psychiatric treatment. Indeed, if people find the first hallucination pleasant, they typically want it to happen again.

How they happen

Many scientists think that normal perception starts with the brain creating a prediction of what is 'out there'. This prediction is then revised using feedback from the world, and forms the basis of what we perceive. Perception is edited hallucination.

So one way to understand hallucinations is as uncorrected predictions (my recent book explains this in more detail). If someone has been a consistent, valued presence in your life, the brain is so used to predicting them that it may continue to do so, overruling the world.

A new day has come, but the brain still bets on yesterday.

Don't judge

Why don't we hear more about these experiences? The obvious answer is that hallucinations are often stigmatised. In countries such as the UK and US, people are typically taught that they are a sign of madness.

So it is perhaps unsurprising that a study in the UK found that only 28% of people with bereavement hallucinations had told someone else about them. Not one had told their doctor. Although most could give no reason for why they had not told anyone, those who did most often cited a fear of ridicule.

This problem is not apparent in all countries. For example, a study in Japan found that 90% of widows felt the presence of their dead spouse, yet none worried about their sanity. Ancestor worship may help Japanese people mourn.

As a result of all this, people should think twice about judging these experiences harshly. One study of widowed people found bereavement hallucinations only occurred in those whose marriages had been happy; we should perhaps simply be marvelling at the power of love.

19 July 2017

⇨ The above information is reprinted with kind permission from *The Conversation*. Please visit www.theconversation.com for further information.

Facebook friend requests from dead people hint at horrifying truth of 'profile cloning'

It's not just dead people's accounts that could be compromised.

By Andrew Griffin

It's horrifying enough to have to deal with a person's social media accounts after their death. That's without the added stress of having that same account appear to be active.

Facebook users have reported receiving friend requests from accounts associated with dead friends and family members. And aside from the obvious distress such a request can cause, it also points to a worrying scam that affects people on Facebook.

Such requests appear to be the result of cloning or hacking scams that see criminals try and add people on the site, and then use that friendship as a way of stealing money from them or running other cons.

Such scams work either by cloning an account – stealing the information from someone's profile and then using it all to set up a new account that is actually controlled by someone else – or by hacking into and taking control of an old one.

Both techniques give scammers the ability to send messages, posing as someone's friend. Once that happens, a range of different hoaxes, cons and scams are possible.

Those might include tricks such as the 'friend in crisis' scam, where a person claims they are stuck somewhere and need money to get out of a problem. Or they might be as simple as using the account to send a link in a message, which appears genuine but in fact forces a user to download problem malware. Or the fake account might never get in touch at all, instead using

the account to look at a person's statuses and other information to impersonate them or steal from them.

There's nothing special about dead people's accounts that makes them more susceptible to cloning or hacking. The same tricks can happen with people who are still alive, and so it is worth rejecting and reporting any friend request that seems suspect or not genuine.

But because of the sensitive nature of the account, and the fact that it is obviously shocking to receive such a request, it can be more obvious that an account has been cloned if such a message is received. And because the person is no longer around to log in to their account, the chance that it will be hacked and not discovered is increased.

Facebook's help forums are filled with people reporting that they have received friend requests from the accounts of dead people. Some of them appear to be newly created, cloned accounts, while others appear to be requests from people's real –but now hacked and taken over – accounts.

'Someone has stolen the account of a friend of mine who died several years ago,' wrote one user. 'They asked me to friend them and, obviously, this person can't be contacting me unless they have Facebook in heaven.'

On one of those posts, a member of Facebook's help team encourages a user to submit a request to have the account memorialised – Facebook's special tool to have a profile turned into a place to remember its owner, rather than an active account– or to have it deactivated entirely, so that it can no longer be used.

10 April 2017

⇨ The above information is reprinted with kind permission from *The Independent*. Please visit www.independent.co.uk for further information.

© *independent.co.uk 2018*

What happens to your digital assets when you die?

From banking and social networking to storing pictures and listening to music, we can do everything digitally these days. But what happens to these digital assets and online accounts when we die? Moneywise investigates.

By Helen Knapman

Just one in four (23%) adults has organised their financial information well enough to allow their loved ones to handle their financial affairs relatively easily on death, while more than one in ten (12%) admitted that it would be very difficult for anyone to handle their financial affairs after they died.

These were the findings of research published earlier this year by financial provider Royal London. But to complicate our financial information further, we now live in a digital world where paper trails aren't left as handy clues for executors trying to sort out the wishes laid out in wills.

Gary Rycroft, a partner at Joseph A. Jones & Co Solicitors in Lancaster, explains: 'Back in the day, it was easy for executors to track down assets as there was physical evidence such as paper bank statements and share certificates.

'While the legal advice hasn't changed in needing to make a will, you need to expand on it and think about what life entails now.

'The big issue that the digital world throws up is that people don't know where to look – it's just a black hole. Where are people's online bank accounts?'

However, it's not just the obvious financial accounts, such as your online banking or share trading and investment accounts that you need to consider. There are also the accounts that aren't financial but still have a monetary value, such as loyalty schemes and cashback sites. According to cashback website TopCashback's *Loyalty after Death* report published this spring, 60% of people have not made their family or friends aware of the loyalty programmes they belong to.

The report also revealed that the majority (91%) of people do not have a plan for their loyalty schemes, and nearly half (47%) had not even considered it as an option.

It's a similar story when it comes to social media accounts. Unless you're an Instagram or YouTube star these are unlikely to have a monetary value, but it's still a personal choice as to whether to keep these open, and not enough of us are recording these decisions before we pass away.

James Norris, founder of The Digital Legacy Association, a professional body that works with charities and organisations to raise the quality of end-of-life care in areas relating to digital assets and digital legacy, says: 'The ways in which we remember our loved ones has changed. For many people, Facebook and other social media sites become a focal point where we remember, view photos, and discuss the life of our loved ones.'

Yet, according to The Digital Legacy Association's *Digital Death Survey 2017*, only one in ten (13%) has made plans for their social media accounts following their deaths.

What happens to your digital assets

Once they have found your digital assets, it's up to executors of your will (or administrators if there is no will) to ask providers and financial institutions to close any online accounts you have, with any remaining balances or assets distributed according to the will if there is one, or according to intestacy rules if there isn't.

Executors will probably need to provide evidence, such as a death certificate and/or a probate certificate. But the problem is that every provider has different rules.

When it comes to banks and building societies, for example, the largest firms follow the 'Bereavement Principles' – a code of practice drawn up alongside industry trade bodies.

Under this guidance, a one-stop notification system enables providers to notify relevant brands about specific accounts and products under the deceased's name with one single notification.

Upon notification, restriction to sole accounts is limited to the person responsible for dealing with the estate. Assets will be released once all supporting documentation to confirm the death and the appointment of the executor or administrator has been provided (although firms will allow payments to be made from the deceased's account beforehand to cover funeral costs, probate fees and inheritance tax payments to HMRC)

Loyalty providers, meanwhile, can set their own rules on whether points or cashback accrued can be passed on when you die.

Leigh Sagar, a barrister at New Square Chambers in London and member of STEP (the Society of Trust and Estate Practitioners), explains: 'In legal terms, a consumer is entering into a contract with a company when joining a loyalty programme. The contract is not an onerous one, but it does contain certain terms and conditions that will be enforced by the court. These terms normally provide that only the registered user, or in some cases, persons in the same household, can collect and spend loyalty rewards.'

Six out of seven major providers Moneywise spoke to do allow loyalty points and outstanding balances to be transferred to someone else, but even then the executor often must provide legal documents to validate their claim

Provider	Can you transfer loyalty points or account balance on death?	Additional information
Avios (formerly known as Airmiles)	No	While Avios' Ts&Cs state that unused points are cancelled after a member's death, it told Moneywise it will consider transfer requests on a "case by case basis"
Boots Advantage Card	Yes	Evidence isn't required but certain security questions will have to be answered
Nectar	Yes	Whether evidence is required depends on whether the executor is an additional cardholder on the account and how many points have been collected
PayPal	Yes	What evidence must be provided depends on whether the account balance is above or below £5,000. As a minimum, a copy of the will is needed (if there is one), plus an original or certified copy of the death certificate, and government-issued ID of the executor or administrator
Quidco	Yes	Death certificate and letter of probate must be provided. Any balance is lost if an account is dormant for six months
Tesco Clubcard	Yes	Evidence isn't required
TopCashback	Yes	Death certificate or will must be provided

Source: Moneywise, 9 November 2017

and some providers will wipe balances if you don't act fast enough (see table above).

How to protect your digital assets

The least you can do to help your executors with a potentially tricky journey ahead is to provide a roadmap of what you want to happen when you die. Mona Patel, Royal London's consumer spokesperson, says: 'While it's not nice to have to think about dying, the last thing you would want is for your family to struggle to locate and deal with your assets.'

Mr Rycroft's advice is to make a will stating how you want your financial assets to be distributed, and who you want to do this. He then recommends writing a digital directory that is kept with your will where you detail every online account you have stating: the website address, your username, and your instruction upon death, e.g., close the account.

'This isn't part of the will,' says Mr Rycroft. 'But it should be kept with the will. It's a living document as it gets updated all the time whereas wills you might make every ten years. So you need to keep a copy at home and regularly update and review it.'

However, he warns that you shouldn't write down passwords as that's a security risk.

You also shouldn't log in to someone's accounts or computer using their details as this is a criminal offence under the Computer Misuse Act 1990 according to Mr Rycroft.

Digital downloads can't be passed on

Sadly, not all digital assets can be transferred in their digital format. Mona Patel, Royal London's consumer spokesperson, explains: 'Many people might be surprised to learn that purchases such as e-books and digital music cannot be passed on, as the

right to access them lies only with the owner.'

Solicitor Gary Rycroft adds: 'With downloaded items, such as films and music, you're buying a right to listen to the music for the duration of your life, but you can't assign that right to anyone else on your death.'

This may hit millennials particularly hard, with Royal London estimating that over the course of a lifetime, someone aged 34 today could build up a digital legacy worth up to £7,700 which cannot be passed on to friends and family.

However, there is a way around this. Mr Rycroft explains that if you download the films, music or e-books onto an external hard-drive, MP3 Player or Kindle, you could then pass on this tangible asset. You're not however, allowed to pass on these assets digitally – say via email.

7 December 2017

⇨ The above information is reprinted with kind permission from Moneywise. Please visit www.moneywise.co.uk for further information.

Moneywise Personal Finance Teacher of the Year Awards

Every year Moneywise awards thousands of pounds of prizes to schools around the UK where teachers undertake brilliant personal finance teaching for their students.

Teachers can enter themselves, or students can nominate them, by emailing editor@moneywise.co.uk explaining why they should be nominated for the awards. Nominees will be contacted for further submissions in the Spring.

Key facts

- Life expectancy. 82.3 years for men and 85.8 years for women. (page 5)

- Healthy life expectancy. The age up to which people can expect to live healthily is 63.1 for men and 63.7 for women. (page 5)

- 70% of people would prefer to die at home. (page 16)

- The cost of a basic funeral, which makes up 46% of the total cost of dying (up from 44% in 2016), has risen by 4.7% from £3,897 in 2016 to £4,078 in 2017. (page 18)

  - This figure is calculated by taking the combined average cost of cremations and burials; the average cost of a burial in 2017 is £4,561, which is almost £1,000 (£965) more than the average cost of a cremation – £3,596. (page 18)

- The cost of a burial has risen by 4.7% in the past year and by 116% since SunLife began tracking costs in 2004. (page 18)

  - The cost of a religious burial is even higher. The average is £4,715 which is more than two-and-a-half times what it cost in 2004. (page 18)

- If funeral costs continue to rise at the same rate we have seen over the past decade, the average funeral will cost almost £5,000 in five years' time. (page 18)

- If wages had risen in line with funeral costs, the average weekly wage would be £714 today, but in reality, it is £503. And if the cost of bread had risen at the rate of funerals, it would now cost £1.52 for a 800g loaf rather than £1.03. (page 18)

- Even house prices have only risen at a third the rate of funerals; today, the average house price is £223,257, but if house prices had risen in line with funerals, the average home would now cost £94,696 more, an average of £317,953. (page 18)

- In 2017, 25% of funerals were burials, 75% were cremations and of those cremations, 3% were direct cremations. (page 19)

- Burial costs differ hugely across the UK. The average cost is £4,561 but in London, the average cost is more than half again at £7,311. At the other end of the scale is Northern Ireland, where the cost of a funeral with a burial is £2,895, less than half the cost of one in the capital and 36.5% less than the national average. (page 19)

- An estimated 2.5 billion people watched the funeral of Princess Diana. (page 20)

- Cremations account for 70% of all funerals in the UK. (page 20)

- Cremation was made legal in 1902 after 28 years of campaigning. (page 20)

- 27% of people would like a church service with hymns as their send off, while 54% of respondents claimed that they would like a more personal service. (page 20)

- 'Broken heart syndrome' – which can be triggered by severe emotional distress, such as the death of a loved one – may leave longer lasting damage than previously thought, experts have revealed. (page 33)

  - Around 3,000 people per year in the UK suffer from the condition, also known as Takotsubo syndrome, according to the Press Association. (page 33)

  - Figures show that between 3% and 17% of people with the syndrome die within five years of diagnosis. (page 33)

  - Some 90% of sufferers are female and a stressful trigger is identified in around 70% of cases. (page 33)

- According to a British Social Attitudes survey, almost half of people (48 per cent) think that children under 12 should attend funerals, while just over a quarter (26 per cent) believe they should be kept away. (page 34)

- Sensing a deceased spouse is remarkably common. Between 30 and 60% of elderly widowed people experience so-called bereavement hallucinations. (page 35)

- Just one in four (23%) adults has organised their financial information well enough to allow their loved ones to handle their financial affairs relatively easily on death, while more than one in ten (12%) admitted that it would be very difficult for anyone to handle their financial affairs after they died. (page 38)

- 31 million at risk of dying without a will. (page 38)

- The majority (91%) of people do not have a plan for their loyalty schemes, and nearly half (47%) had not even considered it as an option. (page 38)

- Over the course of a lifetime, someone aged 34 today could build up a digital legacy worth up to £7,700 which cannot be passed on to friends and family. (page 39)

Bereavement

To experience a loss; the loss of a loved one through their death.

Cemetery/graveyard

Area of land where bodies are buried (unless cremated) and headstones erected to remember the dead. It is usually found attached to a place of worship or crematorium.

Coroner

A doctor or lawyer responsible for investigating deaths.

Cremation

A method of disposing of a dead body by burning. The ashes produced are given to the family of the deceased, who can either keep them or choose to scatter them, often in a favourite place of the deceased.

Death Café

Where a group can discuss death, drink tea and eat cake. It is generally a group-directed discussion of death with no agenda, objectives or themes. It is a discussion group rather than a grief support or counselling session, although people grieving may find them helpful.

Digital legacy

It is not clear on what should happen to a person's online data when they die. This includes all their online accounts, such as email, banking and social networking sites. This can also have an effect on their digital assets, such as music, films and even computer game character – who has the right to decide what will be done with them? Should family members be allowed to have access to them?

Eco/green funeral

People are now environmentally aware and are now opting for 'eco' funerals. This means that people are planning 'green' funerals that will have a minimal impact on the environment, such as a woodland funeral on an eco site. This can involve a coffin that is biodegradable (e.g. cardboard or willow), no embalming or toxic chemicals are to be used on the body or the coffin and often a tree is planted in place of a headstone.

Eulogy

A speech delivered at a funeral, praising the person who has died and reminiscing about their life.

Executor

Someone responsible for the administration of a person's estate after their death, usually nominated by the deceased in their will.

Funeral

A ceremony, often faith-based and held in a place of worship, which friends and family of the deceased can attend as a way of saying goodbye to their loved one.

Grief

An intense feeling of sorrow felt after a bereavement; the process of facing the loss of someone you love.

Headstone

Also known as a tombstone or gravestone. A stone monument erected to a dead person, usually inscribed with their name and dates of birth and death, which friends and family can visit as a way of remembering the dead person. It is usually found in a cemetery.

Living funeral

An end-of-life celebration arranged while the person, who is most probably suffering from a terminal illness or has a sense that their time is short, is still alive.

Mourning/grieving

A period during which an individual is in a state of grief. The phrase 'to be in mourning' is more specific – it suggests the observation of certain conventions, for example wearing black.

Post mortem

A medical procedure carried out on a dead body to discover the cause of death where this is unclear.

Undertaker

Also known as the funeral director. A person who is responsible for organising funerals and preparing bodies for burial or cremation.

Widow/widower

A widow is a woman whose husband has died. A man whose wife has died is called a widower.

Assignments

Brainstorming

⇨ As a class, discuss what you understand about death and bereavement:

- What is bereavement?

- What is a widow?

- What is a widower?

- What is a cremation?

- What are digital assets?

Research

⇨ Do some research into the types of funerals on offer in the UK and look at the costs involved in different areas of the country. Prepare a graph to show your findings.

⇨ Prepare a questionnaire for your family and friends. Have they considered what type of funeral they would prefer? Do they have a favourite song they would like played? You should ask at least seven questions. Write some notes on your findings and share with the rest of your class.

⇨ In pairs, choose a country other than your own. Do some research into funeral practices in that country. Write a report on your findings which should cover at least one side of an A4 sheet.

⇨ In pairs, do some research into what happens to social media accounts when someone dies. Write a report and feedback to your class.

⇨ Do some research into digital assets. What are digital assets? You should consider the different types of digital assets people have and how these might be accessed after their death.

Design

⇨ Design a leaflet about bereavement informing people of the help which is available to them.

⇨ Imagine you work for a funeral director. Design a poster advertising the services they offer.

⇨ Look at the illustration on page 23 and design your own illustration to replace it.

⇨ In small groups, design an app which will allow students to gain confidential advice about how to deal with grief.

Oral

⇨ In small groups, discuss the issue of taking children to funerals. What age do you think it might be appropriate for them to attend? How do you think a child could be prepared for this event?

⇨ Divide the class in half. Debate burials versus cremations. One group should argue for burials and the other for cremations.

⇨ Choose one of the illustrations in this book and, with a partner, discuss why the artist chose to portray the article in the way they did.

⇨ Read *Cost of Dying Report 2017* on page 18. Create a PowerPoint presentation that explores the costs involved.

Reading/writing

⇨ Write a one-paragraph definition of the term 'profile cloning'.

⇨ Write a one-paragraph definition of 'Cryogenics'.

⇨ Think of a name for a song to be played at a funeral and write the first two lines of it.

⇨ Imagine you are an Agony Aunt/Uncle. A man has written to you and said his wife died six months ago. He is missing her dreadfully and is lonely. He feels that his family do not understand. Write a suitable reply and let him know what help is available.

⇨ Read the book *Hallucinations* by Oliver Sacks, which talks about bereavement hallucinations. Write a review of this book.

⇨ Read the article *20 of the coolest funeral ideas to celebrate life* on page 25. Think of another idea to add to the list.

⇨ Write an article for your school/college newspaper explaining why it's important to seek help if you are suffering from grief and find you cannot cope with your feelings. Include some information about organisations that can help.

⇨ Write an article exploring how the Internet is changing the way in which people grieve. Read the article on page 30 for help.

Acknowledgements

The publisher is grateful for permission to reproduce the material in this book. While every care has been taken to trace and acknowledge copyright, the publisher tenders its apology for any accidental infringement or where copyright has proved untraceable. The publisher would be pleased to come to a suitable arrangement in any such case with the rightful owner.

Images

All images courtesy of iStock except page15, 30, 32 and 34: Pixabay. Page 10 and 11: Unsplash.

Icons

Icons on pages 5 and 6 were made by Freepik from www.flaticon.com.

Illustrations

Don Hatcher: pages 9 & 29. Simon Kneebone: pages 26 & 13. Angelo Madrid: pages 23 & 36.

Additional acknowledgements

With thanks to the Independence team: Shelley Baldry, Danielle Lobban, Jackie Staines and Jan Sunderland.

Tina Brand

Cambridge, October 2018